SHORT of a MIRACLE

TINA TORRY'S STORY OF HOPE IN THE MIDST OF TRAGEDY

Short of a Miracle

Ambassador Emerald International
427 Wade Hampton Boulevard
Greenville, S.C. 29609 U.S.A.

and

Ambassador Productions Ltd.
Providence House
Ardenlee Street
Belfast BT6 8QJ, Northern Ireland

www.emeraldhouse.com

cover design and page layout by A & E Media, Sam Laterza

ISBN 1 889893 69 2

Short of a Miracle

Tina Torry's Story of Hope in the Midst of Tragedy

Crystal Pitrois

AMBASSADOR
EMERALD INTERNATIONAL
427 Wade Hampton Blvd.
Greenville, South Carolina 29609

CHAPTER ONE

One hundred fifty dollars and half an hour. Simple on the surface. It seemed perhaps a little too simple, for in the back of her mind she had the gnawing sense that she should never be driving down that interstate on that day toward the destination she had chosen. But still she drove on, her hands being warmed by the vinyl steering wheel as she gripped the wheel more tightly to stop the nervous shaking in her hands. Maybe she was being a bit melodramatic. It was, after all, a community decision of sorts. Everyone who had encountered her thought the same. This was the best. The only way. She was only seventeen, and seventeen-year-olds were not ready to do otherwise.

She knew that she should probably say something—anything, for the silence would cause too much strain in the growing restlessness between her and her companion. She talked just to drown the oppressing sound of the thoughts in her own head. Thoughts that her confusion prevented her from processing into rational, audible sounds.

Tina steered the car down the interstate. She had traveled the road that connected the city of Spartanburg to Greenville on many occasions. She had journeyed down the interstate with her friends to find adventure, boys, or just to ease the boredom of a restless adolescence. But today, the car was empty, except for Kathy, and the two rode in silence. Today, she seemed suddenly older as an impending decision pressed against her mind. A decision she had technically already made. A decision of which she continued to question the merits in her mind.

She wasn't sure if she had seen another car on the road with her although she was sure she had passed several on this well-traveled stretch. She looked over at Kathy. Emotion overcame Tina as she imagined what Kathy was doing for her just by occupying the seat next to her. Just to hear the sound of her breathing or rather just to imagine the sound of her breaths muffled by the sound of the car engine. Together on a sort of journey unknown. Kathy, merely a distant cousin of her boyfriend, seemed strangely enough at that moment more of a blood sister with this event being the means through which they would be forever bound.

She had not remembered passing the hospital or the other markers that she had written down in order to direct her to her destination. She had recalled them photographically picturing every landmark in her mind as the receptionist described the street, the house number, and the description of the house.

The numbers on the front of the house seemed strangely large. "There it is," she said. Perhaps aloud, perhaps to herself. "There's the street," she repeated. The rumbling that had begun as a vague feeling in the pit of her stomach had moved into her chest as if her heart were a hammer pounding against the walls of her womb.

She had the urge to keep driving. To continue down the street. Continue over to her favorite store to do some shopping. Pretend as if she had never driven on that street or pretend as if she had turned onto the street merely as a short cut. But she was much too brave to run or maybe in another sense much too cowardly or, more accurately, much too young to know where to go or what to do when she arrived there.

The house had once been a residence. For a split second, she could have been lulled into a false sense of warmth in imagining a similar mill house she passed on occasion. For a split second, she could have imagined a bicycle leaning against the house or a wading pool in the front yard. For that split second, she could have seen another vision of the house and what it had once been, but as she pulled closer, she saw the parking lot adjacent to the front lawn and was instantly reminded of the reason she was traveling down the street that spring day on April 4, 1978. As she signaled to turn into the parking lot, she thought one last time of turning around and because she could think of no other feasible answer other than to make the turn, she took a deep breath and pulled into the drive leading to the parking lot to the right of the house.

The typical South Carolina spring sun cast its rays blinding her eyes preventing her from seeing as she squinted toward the sign planted in the front yard just beside the driveway. She continued forward, the trees shading her eyes, the sign finally coming into view. The sign seemed harmless and so did the house, but the feelings she was experiencing were anything but innocuous, and the closer she came to walking through the door of this clinic that had once been a house, the more she felt the dread of what would happen once she was inside.

She had lived with the idea for a couple of weeks that she would be sitting there on that very day in that car in front of the clinic. She had known the minute her period had not come, when the nausea had begun, and when she had confronted her boyfriend and her family with the news.

Since she found out she was pregnant, she had been preoccupied, thinking of nothing but her pregnancy, her baby, and her future. She was reminded every morning when she would awaken to nausea where she would be today and although she had prepared herself, or had attempted to prepare herself, she felt that suddenly the pregnancy had all become new again.

She had never imagined exactly how she would raise a baby. She never thought of how she could feed the baby. She just knew that there was an unfamiliar need inside of her to keep the baby that was still nestled inside her. She could think of no one who would be happy about her keeping this baby. No one but her. She could deal with her own disappointment more easily than she could the dissatisfaction of her family and friends. She had heard all of the reasons as to why carrying this baby to term would be an error. Logic, reasoning, the advice of people who should have known much more about life than she did. It was only her soul and her very being that she couldn't quite convince. The only part of her that wouldn't agree to all of this reasoning was the part of her that seemed to speak the loudest, the part she couldn't silence.

As Tina moved her hand to turn off the ignition, somehow she had a sensibility somewhere, maybe a natural, human one that was telling her how considerable this moment would be in the scheme of her life. She took another deep breath, stepped out of the car, and walked to the door of the clinic.

Tina held the door for Kathy and followed her inside. The old wooden floor creaked beneath her feet as she walked to the receptionist's desk. The odor of antiseptic filled the air, the fumes of the clinic coated her throat as she inhaled.

"Yes?"

"I have an appointment."

"Name?"

"Tina Cook."

"Have a seat and fill out these papers." The receptionist didn't look up as she spoke. She handed Tina the pen and clipboard. The clip was bulging with papers.

Tina took the clipboard and took a seat next to Kathy. The informational part was standard. Name, address, medical history. It was all very clinical. Medical. Sterile. Impersonal. She rifled through page after page until she had completed all of the blanks. Then came the release forms that all the patients had to read and sign. The print was minuscule. She squinted for several minutes attempting to adjust her eyes to the size of the words. The print was illegible, small legalese. She searched through the pages to find some reassurance about what they were about to do to her until after only a few short minutes, she gave up. *All routine*, she thought. Nothing that she needed to read. Just some papers to put in the file. This was anyway a doctor's office, a clinic. What could possibly be harmful, and if there were potential consequences, the doctor would certainly discuss them with her.

What she really wanted more than anything was to get through this clinic visit and put this day behind her. She only knew that when she left that little brick mill house, everything would be different. She would be safe again. She wouldn't have to be afraid anymore because everything would be taken care of. Everything. She exhaled loudly and signed her name on the signature line. She walked over to hand the paperwork back to the receptionist.

"One hundred fifty dollars." Tina pulled the wadded bills from her back pocket. She smoothed the bills, counted them, and held the money in her hand toward the receptionist. "Cash only," she had been told on the phone. The receptionist flipped through the papers to be sure they were signed and then placed them in a folder. She took the money from Tina, placed the bills neatly in the drawer, wrote out a receipt for the payment, and handed the proof of payment to Tina.

"Take a seat," she said when Tina remained at her desk. *What will they do?* she wanted to ask. *What will happen to me? What will they do and how will I feel during and after? I will no longer be pregnant but how? Could I die? Do I need to be afraid? Will I feel the pain?* She had questions shooting through her mind, bouncing off each other, multiplying as they were left unanswered. No one who had told her she should be there had told her what to expect. They just told her it had to happen. It would be a simple procedure. No problem. Simple. The questions to which she would never have a response remained in her mind as the unwritten oath in the room seemed to be to stay quiet. There was too much silence. Too little eye contact. Almost as if everyone in the room was denying to themselves that they were actually there — including the receptionist.

Tina found her seat next to Kathy. She looked over at her. She wanted to put her head in her lap. To cry. To ask her to hold her. At least hold her hand. She looked around at the other faces. Many of them girls like her. Many of them women. Women in their thirties who had the same childish look of unfamiliarity. Women filled every available seat that morning. Twenty-five maybe thirty, all awaiting their turn. Silently awaiting their abortions. The quiet of the room was the most remarkable trait of the clinic. The silence of the women, the silence of the receptionist, the silence of the floor as the creaking stopped when Tina took her seat.

Tina's eyes timidly glanced once again around the room. Her final survey of the room was instantly interrupted by a woman with her hands folded, an inexpressive look on her face. The woman's hands were neatly placed in front of her protruding stomach. A stomach that obviously carried a baby inside. She was maybe six months pregnant Tina imagined. She looked down at her own stomach barely bloated from the regular changes of an early pregnancy but no obvious signs that she was carrying a baby. But this woman, she was pregnant. She couldn't be in the clinic for the same reason as the other women. She had a baby inside her. Tina never looked at the woman again.

She instead thought of all the other girls she knew who had had abortions. Abortion? It's nothing. She had known a girl who had had ten abortions and she had lived through them. She seemed fine. She never talked about the horrors of abortion. The procedure must not have been terribly scary. Otherwise, she would not have suffered through ten abortions. On the other hand, none of the girls she knew had said anything positive either. They generally relayed the information in a furtive whisper or she had heard the news about their abortion through their friends, the girls themselves remaining silent. Perhaps their silence had begun in that very room in that very clinic.

The nurse called her name. She had to swallow hard to choke back the tears. She couldn't look the nurse in the eye. She wanted to run. She didn't want this. Something inside was pressuring her to escape. She couldn't go through with this. But the nurse was holding the door. Holding those papers she had already signed. Her stomach began to rumble as she thought of what those papers could have said. It was too late. She had signed them. No turning back. Kathy touched her arm as if to jolt her into reality. "They're calling you, Tina."

"I know."

The nurse led her back to a bathroom. "We need a urine sample." Tina dutifully followed the nurse's instructions. Urine sample. Have a seat. And then the silence. No reassuring words. No warm touches on the hand. Still the methodical, clinical coldness.

"The test is positive. You're pregnant." Tina wanted to say she knew she was pregnant. After all, wasn't that why she was there in the clinic? The nurse handed her a blue pill and a little cup of water. The powder of the pill was bitter in her throat, the water warm. She swallowed hard again trying to make the pill go down and trying even harder to keep the sobs at bay.

"The doctor will be in shortly. Undress and put on this gown."

Tina slipped off her faded denim jeans and her cotton shirt and placed the paper-thin gown around her. The coolness of the cotton made her shiver. She was no longer sure of what she was feeling. She was hopeful that when the little blue pill took effect, she would feel better. She would be able to forget or even if she couldn't forget, she would at least care less. The minutes ticked by and the euphoria Tina had expected from the little blue pill never came. No numbness. No calm. Just the same unfamiliar fear that riveted her every thought and movement.

Tina walked around the small room. The walls were bare and white. The room consisted of a metal table with stirrups attached to it and a machine. She walked closer to the machine studying more closely the little cup attached to a long tube with a hook-like blade on the end.

The nurse startled her as she reentered the room. "Lie down on the table." Tina obeyed still waiting for the potency of the blue pill. The doctor entered the room just behind the nurse and nodded. The silence. Nothing was said. Nothing. The nurse on her left, the doctor at her feet. A large machine separating the two of them.

The doctor picked up the blade with the tube running back to the machine to the cup that Tina could no longer see. Tina turned her head away but by some sort of impulse turned back to the doctor. She shifted her eyes from the machine, the doctor and the machine, to the nurse. The nurse was watching the doctor. Why would she not look her in the eye? She needed a glance, a smile, or even a word. Tina tried to find some solace by looking out the window. She tried to shift her mind to the horses. *This would be a good day to ride.* She began to imagine herself perched atop a horse, the gait of the horse leading her through the pastures, the spring wind blowing on her face.

The dry coldness of the tube made Tina jump. Suddenly she felt a jab from the tube and a vacuum, a vacuum that it seemed was sucking her entire body into the cup attached to the machine. She looked over to try to see the cup. The machine hid it from her view. Dark red filled the tube. *My baby*, Tina thought. She grimaced and looked at the doctor. His hand rotated and maneuvered the tube through her body, stripping out the contents of her womb. Tina looked again at the tube connected to the cup that held the contents of her body, her baby. The pain ripped through her abdomen and seemed to diffuse throughout her body.

She thought she was dying and she thought she said it aloud. She meant to say it. She tried to say it. She had to stop the doctor before she died. She couldn't form the words. The pain was too great. She tried again to say the words, but the grunts were inaudible over the sound of the vacuum. The machine that was draining her body.

The doctor abruptly stopped the machine.

"Empty your bladder."

Tina thought he was angry with her. Had she done something wrong? Had she said something? The nurse helped her down from the table and directed her to the bathroom just in front of the table. Tina could barely walk. Her head was spinning, her knees wobbled, and her feet were barely able to move. "I think I'm dying." She was sure she had said it this time, but there was no response just the urging of the nurse to empty her bladder. Tina sat on the toilet feeling that she had nothing left inside of her to empty. She had felt the machine ravage her body and now she was dying. She tried to think of John,[1] but her mind raced back to the painful ache in her body. She put her head down on her knees. The nurse came into the bathroom and urged her to get up. The doctor needed to finish. Tina didn't want to finish. She wanted to lie down. She wanted to go home but she was dependent on the nurse to hold her up and help her onto the table. "I think I'm dying," she said again to the doctor but before the word dying came out the vacuum drowned out the sound of her voice. Tina could no longer look at the contents of the tube for nausea began to overtake her.

The pain was unbearable and seemed to continue for an eternity. The sound of the vacuum rang in her head. Her vision was blurred with the sight of the doctor rotating his hand, intruding and prodding into her body until he finally stopped and in a frustrated voice, he said, "It's finished." He had finished. She was now to leave. To go. His part was over. His task complete. She was to go to the recovery room and recover. Recover from the pain. Recover from the sadness.

---

1 The name has been changed.

The room was filled with little white cots. She remembered a movie she had seen about war. About wounded soldiers lying on the cots shivering and moaning and begging for some relief. This room was the same only these women were not soldiers. They were girls and women. Cramping and frowning from the pain. The pain of having their babies stripped from them by the machine. Tina was afraid. Even more afraid than when she had entered the building. The unknown had been better than knowing. Knowing the pain of the machine, the cramping, the pain of knowing what she had done. She didn't know why she felt guilt, she only knew that she did. She looked at the seven other cots in the room. Women alone, lying there, their knees hugged to their chests. Tina began to cry. She wasn't sure why. She was crying from the pain, the physical pain and a pain that wasn't so physical. One that was in her heart. She wasn't sure why but she had an unusual empty feeling like the machine had not only taken the baby from her, but something else that she didn't recognize.

She hoped they were all happy. The woman at the health department, John, her mother, her father, her friends. They had all made it sound so easy. Get an abortion. It had seemed as harmless as taking a pill or as if an abortion would be just a quick trip to the doctor's office. It hadn't been quite so simple at all. The people who had made everything seem so simple were nowhere around to comfort her. Just the women. Alone.

Where were the men? She had seen some men waiting in cars outside with their arms hanging out the open car windows. One of them leaned back taking a nap, another pacing in the parking lot smoking a cigarette. She wondered if they knew that their girlfriends or wives, the women they loved, were in pain. Tina thought of John. "You have to get an abortion. You have to. There's no other way. It'll ruin your life if you have a baby now. It'll ruin my life. We're not ready to be parents. I have things I want to do with my life and you aren't going to ruin my plans with a baby. You're only seventeen, Tina."

"Here. You can take my car." She had wanted him to come with her just to hold her hand so she wouldn't be alone. If ever she had needed him, it was at that very minute, and he wasn't there. She had thought that they had something special. She was no longer sure. She knew that after what had just happened, things would never be the same between them again. She hated him for not being there and at the same time, she would give anything not to be alone. Alone. In a room filled with women like her, she had never felt so alone in her life.

CHAPTER TWO

In between moments of watching nurses come in and out, moments of continuing the hopes that the little blue Valium would finally take effect, she wondered when all of this had happened. When had her life turned so strangely wrong so quickly and at so young an age? She attempted to decipher the moments in her life and how they had culminated to bring her here in this room, one of eight women lying on a cot, a young woman trying desperately to think of something else, anything else, other than her pain.

The questions she had been harboring in her mind about the abortion had transformed into questions she needed to answer as urgently about what events had led her to the abortion clinic. She laughed nervously at the irony. Since she was thirteen, she had been sexually active. For four years she had lived recklessly not using any forms of birth control. After all the times with all the guys, she had never imagined she could become pregnant. Thirteen seemed so young to her as her own ripe age of seventeen had, as a result of the visit to the clinic, all at once seemed much too young chronologically for her mental age.

She had begun the cycle of promiscuity while vying for the attention of a neighborhood boy. Her friend liked him, too. One of the most sacred acts of her life was on a whim at thirteen on a day after school when she was alone. Once again alone. Banished from her father's house, her horses, and what she knew as her home. She had been sent to live with her mother as punishment for some reason, she had never remembered why. And she did what she wanted. Her mother consumed with sadness over the divorce, her father preoccupied with his business and the steady stream of girlfriends that came in and out of Tina's life not much differently than they had disrupted her life before the divorce. Before the divorce, there were many nights that her mother would pack the kids in the car driving from motel to motel, always the same ones. Driving behind the tears and obsession of where her husband was and with whom he was spending his evenings because he wasn't spending them with his wife and children. Through all the turmoil, Tina found herself searching for love and thought she would find the most intimate of loves by giving the most intimate part of herself at the most inappropriate of times.

The way she had felt after giving herself to that boy was not a feeling that she had ever wanted to have again. It was as if one of the most hallowed moments of her life had passed in a flurry as if she were somehow caught in a whirlwind from which she could not escape. She wanted to take it back. To say it hadn't happened. She wanted to go back to get rid of the guilt that she felt. She knew it had been all wrong. She hadn't been able to stop herself. She wanted to win the boy's affections. She failed and, at the same time, she had given up a part of her that she would never be able to get back. No matter how much she wanted to have her innocence returned, she had given it away as if tossing it into a wastebasket. And all the while, she lost the boy. The very one that she gave so much to have, she lost.

No matter how much guilt she had felt the first time, she had somehow pushed the remorse aside. She had begun a pattern she could not seem to halt made worse by her dabbling in drugs and alcohol. She had a void in her heart that she was incapable of filling and, although she had tried to fill her purposelessness with sex and drugs, she found that these behaviors only gave her even more of a drive to fill the hole that was eating at her soul.

Tina's thoughts were interrupted by the sound of another woman entering the room with the same afflicted expression. Her face produced the same wince of pain as she lay down on her cot next to Tina's. Tina wanted to say something to her like "What's your name?" just to feel a connection to someone. No one spoke. No one looked around even though at that point, they were all certain of what the other had been through. Still the silence continued as it had fallen around her the minute Tina walked into the clinic like the silence of the snowfall as the flakes would pile on top of one another with no sounds to give their warning. Or like the eerie silence that one would hear to demonstrate reverence to the dead or peace to the dying.

Funny, she thought. *Before the clinic, there was no silence. Only advice. Abortion. Everyone said, "Abortion."* She remembered telling her mother. "I'm pregnant." Her dark eyes became darker, her dark complexion paled. Her German accent emphasized every syllable. She remembered the disappointment in her mother's face. She remembered even more vividly the anger in her father's and when she thought of her mother and father, the greatest question she wanted answered was how such a beautiful love story had turned so terribly wrong.

Tina's father had left America for a tour as a Military Police Officer in Germany. He had returned with a beautiful German bride on his arm. An olive skinned brunette with coffee-colored eyes found herself swept away by the American. So swept away and so ready to escape from her overbearing father, she had not thought of what she would do in an entirely new culture. She was lost in a place where communication, the very basis of her ability to connect with other people, confounded her. She was in a place where she knew no one and she became completely dependent on a man whom she had scarcely met and married. She had vowed to spend her life with a man with whom her own father forbade her from spending her wedding night. In spite of all the hardships she faced in a new cul-

ture, or maybe because of these very hardships, she threw herself obsessively into her role as wife and mother. She gave him
five children and viewed him as the anchor that connected her
to the new culture in which she was narrowly surviving.

The nurse came in to check and release another woman.
Another woman replaced by another. Tina's feelings alternated
between rage and sadness. She couldn't decide if the anger was
directed toward someone or simply toward the situation she was
hopelessly trying to rationalize in her mind. She continued to
let her thoughts rumble through her head. Had she been
allowed to be a child, be disciplined as a child, be protected as a
child, her fate would have unfolded differently, she imagined.
She would have found love in the stability and warmth of the
arms of her father and mother; the people who were for whatever reason chosen to protect her, to feed her, not just her
stomach, but to feed and nurture her soul.

What had outwardly seemed a conventional childhood was
in fact a tremendously awkward one. Awkward in the sense
that Tina had known there was something very wrong about
the way events developed around her, but conventional in the
egocentric way that all children believe their lives are common-
place. She couldn't deny that there were the normal fond
moments of childhood. She remembered in New Jersey the
flashes that gave her the impression that life was good.
Moments that seemed as if her future would evolve in an
uneventful way. The moments she spent sitting on the front
stoop waiting by the empty milk bottles, awaiting the milkman
to exchange the old bottles for the new ones containing the
milk that cooled her throat on the hot days of summer. Full of
sweet, cool, fresh milk that tasted like no other milk she had
ever been able to drink since. She had thought that the bottles
were what made the milk taste so delicious but as she lay on the
cot, she decided that it was just the memory of childhood,
beautifully innocent childhood. Had she tasted the same bottle
of milk that day lying on the cot, she knew that it probably
would have never been quite so sweet and cool.

Then there were the days that she would spend exploring the streets of Elizabeth with her four brothers and sisters. She would feel disproportionately small when she would look over the skyline of her small town up to the majestic shadows cast by the skyscrapers of Manhattan, but when she returned to the steps of her own house, she felt secure. She felt secure in the fact that her mother would be at home waiting for her, her father joining them once his job at the automotive plant was complete for the day.

Her life had seemed stable until the day came when her father grew tired of his nine-to-five job. He was ready to start out on his own. He wanted more. His tenacious spirit and his desire for wealth gave him the courage to move his family down to South Carolina. The textile industry was booming there and he expected to profit from the growth explosion. They packed up their belongings and left New Jersey. As they left Elizabeth, seven-year-old Tina looked behind her out the window of the car as any seven-year-old would at the only home she knew – with sadness about leaving her home coupled with the excitement for the future that her father had promised.

Her father delivered on his promise. Luxury cars lined the driveway of the large colonial home decorated with columns and flanked on one side by a swimming pool and a barn filled with show horses on the other. The children were treated to lavish vacations, and Tina quickly grew accustomed to the wealth and the magnificent opportunities that came to the more financially fortunate.

She grew particularly fond of the horses. When she was a small child, Tina's father had set her on top of a palomino stallion. She had no fear. No inhibition. She immediately trusted the horse. She moved with his movements. She felt herself leading this large beast and as she grew older her love for horses increased. Her passion grew for these animals that were so endlessly loyal. They reminded her of the beauty and innocence in the world. They were her retreat from the turbulent world around her. She would hop on her horse and he would gallop her far away into enchanted pastures and mystical forests far from the perceived fantasy. He would take her from the world that seemed so perfect from the outside when, in reality, her world was all just an amazingly painted portrait of dissatisfaction clouded by the trappings of their wealth. Her father had changed. Everything changed when the money came.

She clung desperately to her passion for her horses. On Saturday, she would ride her horse the three miles from her home to the state park where she and her horse would compete in the shows. She would watch jealously as the other competitors had parents there to unload their horses from the trailer, their parents giving last minute advice, reassuring them as their nervousness for competition was tempered by the warming smile of their mothers or a nudge of encouragement from their fathers. Tina was alone. She was alone with her tired horse, waiting for the competition to start, spurred on by her own desire and independence that she had been forced to develop at twelve when her mother left her home and her father began his life as a bachelor. She took exceptional pride in the fact that she had won ribbons. She had won several and she had won them on her own. She was always on her own. Her brothers and sisters were dispersed by the divorce. Her father was busied with his business and girlfriends. Her mother was so distraught over losing her husband, she became unavailable emotionally and as a result lost the ability to parent her children. Tina was shuffled from home to home — her father's until she was punished there and then to her mother's until she was allowed to go back to her father's. This jumbled existence continued until she was seventeen.

Just after she turned seventeen, her father's business went bankrupt leaving her father penniless. He lost everything. The house, the cars, and worst of all to Tina, the horses. She remembered the day she had to say good-bye to her horse. She was at one with her horse. At one with the sad far away look. She would miss the feeling of controlling him, riding him, as she could not control her own life and her own existence. But

the horse she could control. She could never control the fact
that her father had left her mother. She couldn't control where
she lived or with whom she lived. She could control nothing.
But she could lead the horse. He followed her obediently sending her exactly where she wanted and how fast she wanted
through the pastures, through the countryside, never betraying
her by turning back against her will. When she lost her horses,
she lost the only part of her life that steadied her or that gave
her security.

The moments ticked by slowly. It was always like that, she
thought. The moments with which she would plead to race by
betrayed her by slowing and the moments she could treasure
forever seemed to slip by without even realizing the seconds
were passing. She would be able to leave soon. She would
surely be next. A woman entered the room in a white uniform.
She reminded Tina of the woman from the health department.
She remembered herself walking alone into the health department, panicking, hoping she wasn't right. Perhaps she just had
a stomach virus and maybe she had the date of her last period
wrong. She had after all never used protection and when she
finally had a steady boyfriend, someone she really thought she
had loved, something happened to mess it all up. She wanted
to explain all of this to the nurse at the health department.
She wanted to tell her so that the nurse would know, but she
said nothing only "I think I could be pregnant." She didn't
remember the exact date of her last period only that it had
been a while and she felt sick. Nauseous. All day long. The
nurse met her with the results and said, "You're pregnant."
That's it. "You're pregnant." Like a slap in the face. Pregnant.
"You're seventeen and you're pregnant. Here is a list of the
clinics in your area." "Clinics?" "Abortion clinics. You're pregnant and you're seventeen. You'll need to call the clinic to
schedule an appointment."

She had remembered having the distinct impression that an
abortion was more like popping a pill or erasing a cassette.
Instead, she had experienced a traumatizing fear and excruciat-

ing pain that she was unable to blot out of her consciousness. In all the panic she had felt, she had not once had the time to think of the real reason she was there. The baby the doctor had removed from her womb and the sadness that the realization had given her. There would be no baby. She had wanted that baby. She would have married John had he asked and instead of her lying on the cot in the middle of a recovery room, she would be planning a wedding. A small one without the white dress, but she would have married him. That would have been the right thing to do. Had he asked her, she would have said yes. She would have been thinking of pleasant things like what dress to wear, when to send thank-you notes for all of the baby's gifts, or would it be a boy or a girl? Instead, she was imaging when her cramps would go away, when she would lose the memory of the fear, and at what moment exactly would she feel relief that she had made the right choice and not the wrong one.

She looked at her watch. An hour had passed since they had called her back. Only an hour. She watched as the women and girls entered recovery as quickly as the recovered ones left. Nurses entering, checking each one of them. Releasing them when enough time had passed to assume that their health was stable.

One of the nurses finally walked over to Tina's cot. "Here. I need to check you." The nurse pulled up the sheet, then the gown. "That's funny. You're not bleeding." *That must be a good sign*, Tina thought. She was ready to get out of the recovery room. She was ready to breathe some fresh air. She needed to clear her head of the sterile odor around her. "Here." The nurse handed her two white pieces of paper. One, a prescription for an antibiotic, the other, birth control pills. "Take these." And no more was said. Take the pills and she would be fine.

Tina walked out into the warm spring day. Her stomach cramping, her knees shaking, every step reminding her of where she had just been and what had just happened although she still wasn't completely sure. She threw the keys over to Kathy. She couldn't drive. Tina put her head back onto the headrest and drifted into a state that seemed like sleep.

Certainly not just after the procedure was so fresh, but eventually, she would be able to push the fear aside as soon as she was far from the building and far from the memory of the abortion. She hoped that her body would start feeling normal again. She needed her body to feel normal again. Normal not only to feel relief from the physical pain, but also to feel relief from the unnamed terror inside of her that had numbed her from the moment she had been within sight of the clinic. She had managed to eat lunch with Kathy but her body still carried remnants of the paralyzing fear. She wanted it to go away. She wished it away. She willed it away, but it was there. An emotion so powerful, her memory would never erase the feeling that she had just experienced.

CHAPTER THREE

In the midst of consciously pushing the abortion out of her mind every time it resurfaced into her thoughts, Tina had scarcely noticed the nausea. She had dismissed the strange sensation in her body as a side effect of the antibiotics and when she finished the course of antibiotics, she rationalized that the imbalance inside her was due to the birth control pills.

Her friends had encouraged her to call the doctor all the same. Her malaise was more than likely a result of the pill. Many women reacted to them at least for the first few months, they told her. Maybe the doctor could give her a different prescription. Tina refused to discontinue taking them. She would never go through another abortion. For two months she had relived the memory of the vacuum, the warlike cots, and the pain. She could never tempt even the thought of returning to that clinic. No matter what physical discomfort those pills induced, she would take them. She would dutifully take them until she was no longer able to bear children.

Tina had phoned the doctor. He had suggested that under the circumstances, she should certainly come in for an exam. She had been a little fearful about seeing the gynecologist, her hesitancy prompted mostly by what she had been through two months prior, but she could no longer bear the nausea. She lay down on the exam table hoping the weakness in her stomach would subside.

The doctor promptly entered the room with Tina's chart in his hands. He lifted each paper checking and rechecking her medical history and her test results. He had an air of puzzlement as he slowly put the manila folder on the table beside Tina.

"When is the last time you had sexual intercourse?"

"A few months ago. Not since the abortion. Why?"

"You're pregnant."

"What? But that's not possible! I couldn't be pregnant."

"And you haven't had sexual intercourse since the abortion?"

"No!" Tina was adamant. She and her boyfriend had barely spoken. He was seeing someone else. He had broken it off. She hadn't been with him. She had been with no one. "I haven't had sex since the abortion."

"It appears, then, that you have experienced a botched, incomplete abortion."

"I can't be pregnant. I was there. I had an abortion. I remember the pain. I was there. I know it happened."

"For some reason, the abortion was incomplete. You're going to have a baby. The first thing we need to do is check the health of the baby, and we do that through an ultrasound. We'll know more after that."

Tina's eyes dropped down to her slender stomach. She wasn't showing. She was thin. She couldn't be pregnant. If she were pregnant, she would be practically five months through the pregnancy. She had thought she had gained a little weight but never enough to be five months pregnant.

Tina followed the nurse into the room that housed the ultrasound equipment. The technician prepared her stomach to view her baby. She felt the greasy substance as the woman gently rubbed the part of her body that was carrying her child. Tina shivered.

"There's the baby's heartbeat." Tina desperately searched the screen. She needed concrete proof for the unbelievable fact that the abortion had been unsuccessful but she couldn't recognize anything. She didn't see a baby. She saw a confusing myriad of images that made no sense to her. None of this story made sense to her. The technician showed her the blip that was the beat of the baby's heart. The blip didn't look like a heart to Tina. Just a blip. She saw nothing. She understood nothing. The disbelief persisted as the shock that the pain she had experienced in the abortion clinic had been for nothing. *How could the pain have been for nothing?*

Tina went back into the examining room where she had begun. The doctor entered shortly after, or perhaps the blow had rendered her numb to the passage of time.

"Your pregnancy is considered high-risk."

"High-risk? What does that mean?"

"It means that we will have to monitor your pregnancy very closely. I've never seen a case of an incomplete abortion like this. I have to tell you that the baby that you're carrying could experience a lot of problems."

"What kind of problems? What problems?" *Problems.* She had thought that she had aborted the baby and now the baby would be born with "problems." *How did this happen? Why is this happening?*

"Your baby could be born with abnormalities. It may not even survive. We just need to keep a close watch to be sure that everything goes as smoothly as possible. I would, however, suggest that you see an attorney immediately. You'll need to take all the information you have to the attorney's office with you."

The baby has a heartbeat. You should see an attorney. Take all of your papers to a lawyer. You're still pregnant. The words came like an assault. They came to her like a dream as the waves of sound crashed in her head jolting her far from reason.

How could this be happening? she asked herself again. She had suffered through the abortion. She had been there. She had experienced the pain. The cramping. She had watched as the doctor maneuvered the instrument. She had felt the force of the machine. She had seen the contents of her womb drained from her body. She had been with the other women as they lay on their cots awaiting their release. She had been one of them.

She couldn't still be pregnant. Her stomach wasn't big. She wasn't showing. If she were pregnant, she would be showing, right?

"Not if the baby isn't growing properly." The doctor's response startled her. She hadn't realized she had been speaking. "There seems to be a bit of growth retardation for some reason resulting from the abortion attempt. You do realize that the baby could be born with a number of birth defects. That's why I'm suggesting you take all of your receipts and medical records and see an attorney immediately."

Tina left the doctor's office shaking her head partly in disbelief, partly because of the shock of the truth. How would she be able to tell her parents? Her father was furious that she had become pregnant. She would have to go back and tell him, tell them all, that she had done what they asked. She had experienced the abortion, but now she must tell them that she was having a baby in spite of the abortion. They would all be disappointed in her. They had all made the solution sound so easy.

What had begun as a simple solution was now a situation with the risk of complications she could have never envisioned. She was going to give birth to a baby whether or not she was ready to be a mother. Not only would she be giving birth to a baby, but no one could tell her whether or not her baby would be normal. No one could even tell her if the baby, the baby that she had secretly wanted all along, would survive.

CHAPTER FOUR

"I'm still pregnant."

The shock gradually settled onto her mother's face.

"What? I thought you just had an abortion."

"I did. The doctor said it was botched. He said that this is a high-risk pregnancy and that something terrible could be wrong with the baby. He says I should see an attorney."

"I don't understand."

Tina wanted to scream, "Neither do I." She held back her emotion waiting for her mother's anger to surface.

"Have you told your father?"

"No. Will you tell him? I'm going out for air."

The humid summer air was suffocating. The nausea continued to afflict her. She thought of what her father would say. He would be enraged. She would have never told him. She was too fearful. He was the kind of man to whom no one wanted to break bad news. She paced back and forth along the sidewalk of the apartment complex. Her stomach churned from the nausea and from what she knew her father would say. She stayed outside only briefly. She could no longer control her desire to hear her father's response. She walked slowly back up the stairs to her mother's apartment.

"Did you call Dad?"

"Yes."

"What did he say?"

"He says that he doesn't want to have anything to do with you."

Tina had expected her father's reaction. She had grown accustomed to his rejection, his punishment, and the withdrawal of his love. She had known since the first time he punished her for a minor indiscretion by sending her to live with her mother, her punishment being always to banish her from his presence. He would withdraw from her the very essence of what she needed as a teenage girl — the love of her father. She wasn't shocked by his response. She only felt the rejection that had become a part of her a long time before. That is, she only thought she wasn't surprised until she realized that she had tears rolling down her face.

"Calm down." Tina's mother took her in her arms and gently said, "I bet you're going to have a little girl."

Chapter Five

Tina's eyes widened as she looked at the wall splattered with diplomas and other official-looking certificates. Sally said her father was an excellent lawyer. He was also charitable enough to entertain a visit from his daughter's friend. Tina felt her face redden as she imagined telling her friend's father face-to-face about the abortion. She had spoken to him on the phone, and although he had seemed more fatherly than businesslike, she could only imagine what this man would think of her and the idea that she was a friend of his daughter.

Tina leafed once again through her papers to be sure everything was there. The receipt for the $150 she had paid, the prescription for the birth control pills and the antibiotics, her medical records from Dr. Rubel. Dr. Rubel. Every time she pictured him she heard the words, "Your baby may be born with a number of birth defects."

"Hi, Tina." Mr. Smith walked into the office and came over to shake her hand. Tina stayed in her chair. "What can I do for you?"

Tina tried to remember every detail. She tried to remember to tell Mr. Smith everything. How the doctor had made her empty her bladder in the middle of the procedure, how he had sounded frustrated like he knew something was wrong, how the nurse had seemed surprised she wasn't bleeding. She felt herself blush as she spoke, but she had to tell him everything. Mr.

Smith looked down at his desk as she spoke.
"Here are the receipts and the proof that I was there."

Mr. Smith leafed through the papers letting out an "uh-huh, I
see" after he glanced over her paperwork. "When I called the
clinic earlier to get your records, they said they had misplaced
them. You're not going to get anywhere with this. You just
need to forget it. To pursue this would just be a waste of time."

"But the doctor told me to see a lawyer. I have the proof. I
have the records. I was there. I had an abortion and I'm still
pregnant. I need to take care of my baby. It could be
deformed."

"You'd be wasting your time if you pushed this any further.
I'm sorry."

Tina left the small brick office building once again alone.
She found herself more and more often alone. By now, she
should be accustomed to the solitude she had experienced so
often before. It seemed that her loneliness was more pro-
nounced as she became older and as she began to face such
overwhelming circumstances. The events she was experiencing
were overwhelming for an adult but crippling for a mere child
of seventeen who was alone. Suddenly, she thought she felt the
rare butterfly sensation of the baby moving in her womb. A
smile and then the guilt. The guilt of knowing that she really
was alone and all she had to hold on to was the very child she
had tried to abort.

She paced in front of the window waiting for the social worker to arrive. In one sense, she was frightened at the prospects of
giving up her baby. After carrying her baby for seven months,
she felt a connection with her somehow. Her mother had
already bought clothes for her, her friends had showered the
baby with gifts, and somehow the fact that she would have a
child had become more and more real to her. At the same
time, she had begun to comprehend a bit of the reality that this

baby would need constant care. It would need to be fed. There would be nights of diaper changings and feedings. What would she do with a baby? How could she raise a baby on her own? She would have to quit school, get a job, support her child in every aspect, and no one around her seemed to want to be burdened with the responsibility. First, the advice was to get an abortion. When that option failed, adoption was next. Tina had begun to feel that adoption would be a good answer. She knew that John wouldn't want to be a part of the baby's life, and she was afraid she wouldn't be able to handle everything on her own. She would give the baby a good family, and at the same time, she would be able to give herself a life. She would finish school and maybe even become a veterinarian. She had always wanted to be a vet. With a baby, her dreams would never be realized.

The social worker pulled into the driveway, and Tina tried to suppress her ambivalent feelings. Fear and excitement. Dread and relief.

"Hi. I'm from the Department of Social Services."

"I'm Tina Cook."

"So, you're seventeen and how far along?"

"Seven months."

"You said that you were considering adoption?"

"Yes."

"Why?"

"I'm alone. I have no support. The baby's father is no longer in my life, and everyone tells me I should give this baby up for adoption."

"Everybody? And how do you feel?"

"Alone."

Tina continued to answer the social workers questions, and all her answers came down to one answer. Tina felt alone. She felt she had no help. No support. She felt deserted.

"I need to come back for another interview, but I'll just be honest with you, Tina. I don't think adoption is the right choice for you."

CHAPTER SIX

The endless procedures and doctor visits became tedious as none of them succeeded in proving very much about the health of her baby. It seemed to Tina that each visit and test only left more questions to be answered which in turn led to more tests. Without all of the scheduled appointments, however, her pregnancy would have seemed almost doubtful to her. While most women would talk of the kicks that come in late pregnancy from their healthy babies, Tina barely felt the flutters of the child she carried. Her silhouette was not that of a woman who was seven months pregnant. She wasn't gaining very much weight, and, according to the doctors, neither was the baby.

Tina scanned the walls to see if anything had changed in the much too familiar examining room in Dr. Rubel's office. *More tests.* She wondered why the doctor kept bringing her into the office for more. She had gone through fetal stress tests. She had been through amniocenteses after amniocenteses. None of the tests could prove that the baby was abnormal or that it would even be born alive, but every time Tina would walk through the door of the office, she would secretly hope that this would be the time she would know more, then she would be able to sleep peacefully unlike she had in the months since the clinic. Sitting in the office on that visit, in particular, she especially wanted to hear some positive news, for as the birth of the baby came closer, she became more and more aware of the fear of having a child with deformities, or worse, carrying a child for nine months and leaving the hospital with empty arms.

The doctor's soft tap on the door interrupted her thoughts. "How are you doing, Tina? Is the pregnancy going well for you?"

Tina wanted to shout, *No! It's not going well. Why can't you tell me if my baby will be normal? Why can't you tell me why she survived? Why I decided to abort her? Why is all of this happening?* She suppressed her frustration. "Yes. Fine."

"I'm sorry to tell you that we don't know anything more. We were unable again to obtain any amniotic fluid. I do have some good news. The fetal stress test that we did was negative, so that means the baby doesn't seem to be in any imminent danger. We'll do another one in a couple of weeks just to be sure. There also seems to be a problem with the way the baby is measuring. We discussed the issue of growth retardation, right?"

"Yeah. You mentioned something about that."

"Well, the baby still doesn't seem to be catching up. It isn't as big as it should be and we really can't tell why at this point. We just need to keep a close check and see you back here in a week or so. Any questions?" he asked as he scribbled furiously on her chart. Certainly she had questions — lots of them. Where should she start? How did this happen? Why couldn't you obtain any fluid? She knew the baby was alive, but she could barely feel it. Why? Would the baby make it through delivery?

Those were all the questions she wanted to ask. And then there were the deeper questions. The philosophical ones. The questions that she at the tender age of seventeen was unable to form. Those that haunted her at night, that interrupted her sleep. The questions to which she could only suppose someday to find the answer with the luxury of age and wisdom. She never imagined that she would ever be so wise as to understand the meaning of all of these events. All that she could do was hope. She hoped against hope that the baby she was carrying could go against the odds again, however impossible it seemed, and live.

CHAPTER SEVEN

The monitors were strapped to her torso by a Velcro band. The routine had become all too familiar. Everyone said she was small for thirty-eight weeks, but she felt very pregnant. Tired and pregnant. It was hard to believe that the beep from the monitor was actually her baby's heart beating. Her baby whom she had barely realized was growing inside her had a heartbeat. A steady, strong heartbeat. *Amazing,* she thought.

The nurse reentered the room with a needle in her hand. "This is an injection of oxytocin. It will show us whether or not the fetus is under stress. You should feel some discomfort but not too much."

Tina winced as the nurse stuck the needle into her arm.

"In a few minutes, you should start feeling the contractions."

Tina began to feel her stomach gently harden, and as it did, the heartbeat of her baby began to fade. With every contraction, the sound became more muffled. Her stomach tightened, the beat softened. And as her stomach softened, she would hear the beat again. "A routine test," the doctor had said. She had been through two others just like them to be sure that the baby was not experiencing any stress. It was routine for all high-risk pregnancies like hers. Only this time the results of the test would not be routine. All Tina remembered hearing as she drove herself to the hospital was, "We have to induce."

"Fetal distress." Over and over, the words filled her head. Her biggest fears were being realized. She could lose the baby.

CHAPTER EIGHT

Once again the fetal monitors were strapped to her as the monitor recorded the beeping of the baby's heartbeat. She thought of the baby and what it would be like. Her mother thought it would be a girl. She had been buying pink, frilly clothes since Tina had been seven months pregnant. Her baby could be a girl. She could be a normal little baby girl. She could have two arms, two legs, or she could be born with an arm delivered later. She could be born with mental retardation. She could be born handicapped. Or worse, she could be born dead. Tina couldn't imagine that happening. How could she mourn the loss of a baby she had tried to abort? She tried to concentrate on the pink frills and lace dresses, on ribbons and bows, on the baby she was about to have, on the life that she would have to make for her baby. Alone. John with someone else. Tina with their child.

She drifted in and out of sleep during the night. Between dreams of her baby girl, she heard the beep, beep, beep of her baby's heart as the contractions gently tightened her stomach. No pain. Just the tightening of her stomach. She slept and waited. Waited for the pain of labor, for the time when she would push her baby into the world. Her healthy baby with bright eyes, two arms, and two legs. With five fingers, five toes. Her child.

The sun began to creep up from behind the edge of the window. She continued to feel the tightening in her stomach. The beginnings of labor. The constant beating of her baby's heart. She caressed her stomach and felt the wave of the contraction as her womb became harder and harder and then released itself trying to push this life into existence.

But all at once, the beat was different. The sound of the heart monitor took Tina's breath. One of the nurses raced into the room looking at the monitor, the heartbeat slowing. The beeps coming more and more slowly. 130 to 50. The machine said fifty. There was a look of panic on the nurse's face. Before Tina could ask what was happening, she had oxygen over her mouth. Oxygen pouring into her, the baby's heartbeat remaining the same slow unfamiliar beat. Not like the strong steady beat that had eased Tina in and out of her dreams through the night. That beat had lulled her. This beat frightened her.

The doctor flung open the door. "The baby may not make it. We have to do a C-Section. Get the anesthesiologist." The baby isn't going to make it. The baby. The baby she hadn't wanted. The baby she had tried to abort. The baby that she had grown to love. The baby that had matured inside her. That baby would come to her, but not alive? Tina had no time to ask questions. The room was filled with doctors and nurses. White coats dashing in and out of the room. She was given shots, then more masks. *Please let my baby be OK*, she thought as she drifted into a drug-induced sleep.

Her first vision as she awoke from the anesthesia was the outline of Dr. Rubel as he walked toward her bed. He was shaking his head. "It's a miracle. You have a baby girl. Three pounds and three ounces. The majority of the placenta was gone and there was very little amniotic fluid. That's the reason for the growth retardation."

"Is my baby OK?"

"She's a fighter. She's battling for her life. She's a miracle to have made it this far."

Tina tried to shake the fog of the anesthesia. Her mother was right. It was a little girl.

Chapter Nine

Tina awoke to twenty-four unfamiliar eyes poised toward her. Standing around her bed were men in white coats. They were leaning toward her to get a closer look. Tina felt like an alien being examined by scientists. They were young except for the physician who spoke. They were standing right in front of her discussing her life story as if she weren't there. The botched abortion. The baby living. Their eyes looked at her, and then as if in unison, they would scrawl on their clipboards. Tina wondered what they were writing and why her story was so remarkable. She knew that Heidi was a miracle. The doctors and nurses told her every time they saw her. She couldn't quite understand why they were studying her so intently, writing the details of her life on their clipboards as they squinted their eyes to look at her as if an answer for her situation would come to them if they looked hard enough. Tina squirmed in her bed and winced from the pain of the incision in her stomach. The doctor with the gray hair didn't stop talking. He continued his story using words that Tina didn't understand. Words that frightened her. Words that made her feel uncomfortable. Looks that made her feel like a specimen.

She watched as their white coats finally ruffled toward the door; as if in chorus, they walked out of the room. One by one. Each of them turned back to look at her — once more getting one last look at the woman with the child who had lived through an abortion. Tina, still confused by the haze of the anesthesia and pain medication, rolled over and drifted off to sleep wondering if the eyes had been a dream.

CHAPTER TEN

Tina had not been able to hold Heidi immediately after giving birth to her. The nurses had whisked the baby away to the intensive care unit where she had been ever since. Tina's mother saw Heidi and gave Tina hourly reports on what she looked like and how she was doing. Finally, twenty-four hours after her birth, the nurse entered the room and said, "How would you like to see your baby?" She helped Tina into a wheelchair and rolled her down the hall to the room reserved for the babies who needed constant care. Tina was amazed at the picture in front of her. Little incubators were lined up in rows with tiny babies inside. Doll-like little babies many of whom were fighting valiantly for their lives. Tina could not see some of the babies because the tubes that were supporting their lives were practically larger than their arms and legs.

Tina wheeled herself farther into the neonatal intensive care unit. Babies. Tiny babies everywhere. Babies with tubes pouring out of their mouths, their noses, and their miniature arms. She took a moment to absorb the shock of the picture. She wheeled closer to Heidi. Her eyes stopped on an incubator cradling a baby the size of her hand. She could have held this baby in her hand. "How far along was her mother?" Tina asked.

"Six months." The nurse was maneuvering a tube into the nose of this tiny creature. Six months. Her mind raced back seven months to the clinic. *The woman with the baby in her* stomach. *The woman that was sitting in the clinic. Did she abort her baby? It would have been this big. It could have been born. It could have been lying there in that hospital with tubes coming out of it struggling to breathe, but breathing all the same. The baby in her stomach was like this baby. A tiny little baby, moving, breathing, alive.* Tina swallowed hard as she thought back to what she had had in mind for her own baby. Her little Heidi.

"Heidi is over there."

Tina wheeled over to her baby. Three pounds, three ounces. She was tiny but seemed enormous next to some of the other babies. The doctor had called her a fighter, a survivor. Miracle Baby. She looked so vulnerable and so weak with tubes coming out of her. A tiny little living creature. Her baby. She reached in to feel her skin so that Heidi could feel her mother was there. She needed for Heidi to know that she was there.

CHAPTER ELEVEN

Tina looked over the crib at her delicate little daughter wrapped in a preemie diaper that was still much too large, even with the diaper pinned as taut as possible. The sleeves of her white cotton t-shirt came barely above her wrist, and on her head was a knitted cap someone had made especially for Heidi, for all the normal newborn clothes were still much too large for her. Heidi had fought for a month struggling with the most basic human functions. Tina had watched her struggle to suckle, learning to sustain her small body, as she weaned herself from the feeding tubes. She had watched as Heidi had learned to breathe on her own. She had listened as the doctors and nurses called Heidi, "Miracle Baby". She was a miracle for surviving the abortion but even more of a miracle was the progress she had made in one short month.

The "Miracle Baby" had caused quite a stir in the hospital. Heidi had received constant care, and Tina, flattered by the attention, attempted to interpret all the talk about miracles that had been associated with her pregnancy and the birth of her firstborn child. Heidi's birth had been complex and her recovery had seemed next to impossible, but what exactly did miraculous mean? People told her that her child had been a special gift from God, that God had shielded her from harm. But why? She certainly hadn't understood the concept. The only times she had heard about the existence of God was from her grandmother and a group of men she had never met. Tina's grandmother would visit twice a year, and each time, she would tell Tina that she was praying for her. And then there were the men in the white shirts and black pants on the street corner in downtown Greenville who would call to her and her friends when they were cruising the town to see if they knew someone called Jesus. Her friends had never taken them seriously, but as she looked down at her baby girl, surrounded by the sights and sounds of Christmas approaching, she had the faint impression that there must have been a reason why Heidi had come through so much. But God... Why would He save her baby when Tina didn't believe?

Heidi's birth had seemed so medically impossible to the physicians who had watched Tina's pregnancy and Heidi's birth progress, they asked Tina to participate in a panel to tell her story via satellite to students at a state medical university. She knew on a certain level how important such an event was in the scheme of medicine, but the deeper understanding of how profound an event Heidi's birth was in the medical community confounded the naiveté of a girl barely ready to be a mother. She found unfathomable the idea of a Higher Power intervening in the birth of her offspring.

At eighteen, however, she had enjoyed the attention of telling her story. The novelty was appealing to her quickly fleeting youth as she felt trapped on the edge of adult life, her juvenescence slowly being seeped from her by the demands of caring for a newborn baby with special needs. Coupled with the confusing concept of the divine intervention that had seemed to take control of her life overnight, Tina had not only been called the receiver of a miracle, she had become a mother. A much less mystical role, she found herself hurled into the throes of motherhood. Dirty diapers, late-night feedings, her freedom slashed from her but her youth still pounding inside of her for the freedom she somehow felt she deserved. Tina had a baby to feed, clothe, nurture, and love, and as her own needs had been unfulfilled in her own childhood, she was unsure of how to find the ability to give all the necessary affection that she had scantly received herself.

Upon arriving home from the hospital, her mother had helped a lot with Heidi. She had taught Tina how to take care of a baby. Nothing had come naturally to her. Tina had fumbled over diapers, bottles, and this little person who was so foreign to her. Tina had really never even taken care of herself. She had never lived on her own. She had dabbled in part-time employment, but the needs of a baby required more responsibility and energy than she could find within herself.

Since she had held Heidi in her arms for the first time, her feelings had assumed a sort of frightening and guilt-provoking ambivalence. She couldn't understand nor could she rationalize her feelings. She felt an intense love for her baby, but at the same time, not only did the trauma of the birth play over in her mind, she couldn't seem to shake the immeasurable guilt she was experiencing due to the fact that she had tried to abort her baby, the very baby that she had held in her womb. What should have been a joyous event fixed in time with photographs and birth announcements had been turned into a medical study scrutinized by doctors, studied by interns, and questioned by the mother who wondered why her baby had even survived. All of these emotions churned in her head. She felt out of control and resentful for the idea that this child had come upon her without her being able to control the outcome. Then there were mixed emotions for the father of this baby. Heidi was part of the man who hadn't loved Tina enough to stay, and at the same time, this baby carried a part of him in her.

And why had she survived? These thoughts were the forbidden ones. She knew consciously that she should have never wanted the answer, for wasn't it enough that she had her daughter with her? The daughter that she had almost lost at the clinic and then at birth? Why had this little child conquered so much, and why was she there in the crib next to Tina? She felt she had given too much for a child. With the demands of the child, she couldn't finish high school and fol-

low her dreams. Soon when Heidi was released from her week-
ly doctor visits, she would be forced to find a job, and the
prospects for a high school dropout were less than desirable.
But the hardest part of having a child at such a young age was
letting go of the feeling that she was missing out on so much by
being a mother.

She thought of the evening when Heidi was only a couple of
months old that had been the most tangible result so far of the
loss of her carefree teen years. She had finally met someone
who interested her, and she had been seeing him when she
could, which was always when her mother wasn't too busy to
watch Heidi. He had called to see if she wanted to go to a
friend's house to enjoy an evening of sledding on the freshly
fallen snow. Tina had begged her mother. Her mother's
response was "No, Tina. You have to watch Heidi. I have
some place to be." Tina had sat home alone, feeding her infant,
changing diapers, and then watching her baby as she drifted off
to sleep imagining her friends sledding gleefully down slopes of
snow, squealing with delight at the speed of the sled and the
freedom of flying down the hill, sipping hot chocolate around a
fire, arguing over whose sled was the fastest, whose ride the
most exciting. These were some of the normal, simple thrills of
youth that she would no longer be able to experience, not only
because she had a baby but also because she had experienced
too much to ever be young again in her heart. She would
never again slide through the snow with the unencumbered joys
of youth. She grieved. She grieved for what she had lost and
she grieved for the kind of mother she perceived herself to be
for having such forbidden thoughts about her "Miracle Baby".

She felt overwhelmed and out of control, but most of all she
felt the guilt of having tried to abort her baby, this baby that
was lying there so soundly and peacefully in her crib. She had
seemed so intangible at the time. Tina hadn't been able to see
her. She hadn't been able to touch her. She hadn't been able
to feel her move. Her stomach had not grown very much. But
now that she could see her, she knew what she had done, and

she wondered somehow if Heidi knew. Did she feel the rejection of her own mother? Did she know? Did she feel that Tina had tried to betray her own child with the force of a vacuum in the hands of a doctor? Had she felt that Tina hadn't wanted her? Did Heidi feel her mother's resentment for her baby seizing control of her life and her youth? Did she know or sense any of the negative emotions that Tina tried desperately to suppress but that in the darkest moments in the deep of the night would resurface riddling her heart with guilt? She dared not think that her Heidi knew what she had done, and if she did know, Tina wondered if Heidi would ever be able to forgive her for the ultimate betrayal of a mother to her child.

CHAPTER TWELVE

The clinic was hidden by trees thickly planted on the front side of a large, man-made hill with a tall, brown wooden fence erected on top of the mound of dirt to provide further seclusion. "Are you sure this is it?" Tina asked. "This looks like a military installation."

"There's the sign."

"Women's Clinic."

As they made the right turn into the parking lot, the clinic still hidden by the cluster of trees, Tina saw to her left a large white sign with the words "Free Pregnancy Testing" penned in large black print. The sign was affixed on the lawn in front of a little white house neighboring the clinic. A chain-link fence separated the two properties. The long driveway led them through the large, half-full parking lot. Nestled in the back of the parking lot was a small, wooden house. The neglected state of the old house, the paint cracked and peeling, along with the prison-like mood furnished by the tall, chain-link fence instilled in Tina an uneasy sensation as if she really were entering a sort of military complex.

She looked to her right and saw a second sign. "Obstetrics and Gynecology." *Harmless. A doctor's office. A medical procedure. A choice. Five years ago was five years ago,* she reassured herself. She was determined to suppress the fear that had begun to creep into her consciousness as before, but the more she tried to tell herself she was no longer seventeen, she was a woman, the more she was reminded of all that she had to fear by coming once again to a clinic for another abortion she had never imagined she would once again choose. As Bill[2] opened the door for her to enter the clinic, streams of memories from a clinic five years earlier enveloped her senses sending her reeling momentarily into another time and place. The insecurity. The naiveté. The fear of not knowing what would happen. The silence, the looks, even the odor of the clinic reminiscent of the time when she was seventeen feeling trapped into an abortion against her will.

The receptionist was no less formal and no less methodical. The information was the same as before and, as she hadn't been able to read them before, she had to assume that the waivers were the same as well. She didn't try to read them again. She knew the worst that could happen, she thought. *What else could there be other than what I have already experienced?*

She completed the information, signed the forms, and took her cash once again to the receptionist. She would be paying extra this time. She had agonized over whether or not she should have the abortion. She couldn't shake the memory of the pain. She couldn't imagine feeling the pain of the suction machine again. The mere thought gripped her with terror. She would have never walked again through the doors of the clinic had the nurse not told her that she could opt for anesthesia so that she would feel nothing. Not only would she avoid the physical pain by being under anesthesia, she would also avoid the pain of knowing the purpose of the affliction — terminating the life that was growing inside her.

And then there was Heidi. She had experienced so much fear with her. So many things could have gone wrong. She had the nagging fear in the back of her mind that although next to impossible, she could experience another botched abortion. What if the abortion was again botched and she were left with a handicapped baby? She had learned what could

---

[2] The name has been changed.

have happened when Heidi was born. The baby could have been born with a little arm delivered later. The baby could have been stillborn. Part of the baby could have been left in her uterus potentially causing a life-threatening infection. She knew everything that could go wrong. The logical side of her was sure of the fact that the chances of her having a botched abortion were minuscule. Or were they? She pictured the waivers she had again failed to read. She had lived through the unknown, but she knew that she would rather face more of the unknown than have this baby. She was certain. And so was Bill.

Tina knew from experience that to look around the room would be fatal to the calm she was trying so hopelessly to guard. To look at the faces of the other women would only remind her how confused and sick she felt by being there. She had hoped to look to Bill for solace, but he looked as disconcerted as she did. He didn't feel good about being the only man in a room full of women who were not at ease even among themselves.

Just two short years earlier, she and Bill had been waiting on the steps of the courthouse for the guests of their wedding to arrive. Tina had always imagined her wedding day to turn out differently. More like the fairy tale. She was not the princess bride in the white dress floating majestically down the aisle on the arm of her beaming father. The wedding was instead a gathering of five. The bride, the groom, Tina's mother, Heidi, and Bill's father. Tina's father still refused to speak to her, and Bill's mother was boycotting the wedding out of her disapproval of her son's bride. The wedding consisted of a short ceremony officiated by the Justice of the Peace.

Tina had met Bill through her brother. She had been careful in her courtship. She wanted to be sure she had found a man who would assume the role of a father figure in the life of her daughter. Her marriage would be different from her parents. Her marriage would last, she had promised herself. There would be no infidelity, no lies, no deceit. She had dreams of growing old with Bill, and when they were on their feet, they would take Heidi and start their family.

On their wedding day, Tina and Bill tried to overlook the bitter sweetness, but the idea that they had started their marriage on such a negative tone by having Tina's father and John's mother boycotting the wedding was hard to ignore. They tried to focus on the joy of starting a new life together. Of promising to love, honor, and cherish one another in spite of the obstacles that had already begun to taint their marriage. Tina couldn't help but wonder what had gone so wrong. They had been separated, seeing each other from time to time trying halfheartedly to put their marriage back together amid two lifestyles that were not meant for a married couple with a child. Both of them were deep into their own lives harried by alcohol, drugs, and searching for more than either of them could seem to find, their marriage after two short years had become seemingly unsalvageable.

She and Bill didn't speak. They both looked straight ahead. Tina wondered if he were thinking the same thoughts as the ones that were running through her mind — the thoughts about their marriage and thoughts about Heidi, the irrational fear that this doctor could make a mistake. Bill's brow was furrowed as if he were thinking the same thoughts, but Tina didn't want to ask. Partly because she didn't want to know. Partly because he probably wouldn't tell her now that they were so far apart.

The time in the clinic seemed to stand still. She would have felt just as alone even if Bill hadn't been with her. She was beginning to wonder if it was the very act of abortion that had brought about the sense of loneliness. Although she could rationalize not bringing a baby into the world and explain away the fact that she had seen the results of what abortion terminated, there was something terribly wrong about the feeling she got when she walked into the clinic. The realization was that at seventeen she hadn't been able to pinpoint the feeling. It had seemed like silence at the time. As a woman, it was morgue-like. The death was the death of the babies and the death of the part of the women that they all seemed to know would never live in them again. Different decor, different clinic but the same perception of fear and grief. The fear on the faces of many of the women as they waited. The grief as they filed out.

After a few minutes, a nurse came out to the waiting room and called Tina back. Again the pregnancy test, but this time no blue pill. She wouldn't feel the pain this time. She lay back on the table and waited to drift off to sleep to turn off the feelings. She tried to look straight ahead to avoid looking at the machine. The machine that had caused so much pain to her the first time she was lying on the table. The machine with the tube, the suction, the cup. The cramping, the angry doctor, her feeling so close to death. This was for the best. She knew that when she woke up, she would get up from the table with one less problem with which to deal in her already chaotic life.

When she awoke, she was in the recovery room. Girls were walking around the room crying. Not hiding their tears. They couldn't hide them. Their tears were too real. Their hearts broken. Tina began to wonder if they, too, had felt trapped. Had they aborted their babies like she had the first time? In an effort to make everyone happy? To do what everyone else had wanted them to do? Maybe they were seventeen and felt they didn't have another option. Possibly they had fathers who wouldn't love them if they were pregnant. Perhaps their boyfriends had left them when they found out. Or maybe their husbands had not wanted them to have a child. She wanted to ask them why they were crying. What were their circumstances? Is an abortion not what they wanted? Did they have regrets? She wanted to ask. But she began to think less about the other women when she realized that she, herself, had tears streaming down her face. She wasn't sure why she was crying. She had wanted an abortion. She and her husband had decided. And still, she was crying. She felt relief, and at the same time she couldn't control herself. She should have felt relief. *I'm relieved*, she said to herself, *I'm so relieved. It's done. I don't have to worry about having the baby.* Those words she kept repeating over and over in her head, but she couldn't shake the extreme sadness that had overtaken her. She wept without inhibition. The nurse turned to the other nurse and said in a voice filled with pity or annoyance, Tina wasn't sure which, "She's crying."

Tina wanted to scream, "We're all crying. Why are we all crying?" There was something unnatural about the way she felt. She hadn't experienced that feeling before. It was as immeasurable and foreign a sentiment as she could imagine. It was as if her entire body were filled with sadness, but her conscious mind wasn't in tune to why. Like her body was trying to tell her mind that something wasn't quite right, only it couldn't reach her. She kept talking to her body with logic. Repeating her logic for aborting her child. *We didn't want it. Why would I bring a child into the world when it isn't wanted? It would ruin our marriage. It would be in the way. I don't want a baby. Bill doesn't want this baby either. It's the right thing to do.* She continued repeating the words. Her mind won over her emotions, or she thought that they had. She hadn't really convinced her feelings of anything. She had just drowned them out for the moment so that she could get herself together and get out of the clinic. She would be fine once she got away from the reminders, the triggers, the crying women, the sound of the machine, the smell of antiseptic. The little white cots that harbored the women after the abortion. She would recover. She would make her senses forget and then her emotions would recover, and she would go on as she had done before. She would be able to force recollections of that moment from her mind. She had been able to clear her mind after her first abortion attempt, and this time would be easier. She had become accustomed to the denial. She convinced herself that she would forget. But somehow she hadn't convinced herself enough, for a bit of sadness remained in her heart, and as far down as she tried to push the regret, part of her still felt the sadness that wouldn't seem to go away.

And then there were the thoughts of Heidi. Heidi, now a little girl. She saw her brown vivacious eyes so full of life, yet she had been through so much in her short little life. Tina had endeavored to be a good mother. At nine months old, Heidi had become healthy enough to be able to be put in daycare so that Tina could find a job to try and support her and her daughter. Her neighbor had found a position for her in a local embroidery plant. She had helped out by taking Heidi to daycare and driving Tina to work for six weeks until Tina was able to buy her own car. She had attempted to be a good mother to Heidi, but the remnants of her rebellious youth kept her in the midst of a social crowd that was out of control and a turbulent spirit that refused to be tamed by the needs of her child.

She remembered the day she had gathered the courage to ask her mother if she could move out into her own apartment. Heidi was two at the time and very attached to her grandmother who provided care for her much of the time. Tina and her mother were realistic about the prospects of Tina taking Heidi with her on her own and made the agreement that until Tina was able emotionally and financially to take care of her child, Heidi would stay with Tina's mother. Tina, honest about the way she wanted to live her life, knew that Heidi was in a better environment with her mother. When she and Bill married, however, they both decided to have Heidi live with them. Tina and Bill both adored her, but Tina felt she could never handle another baby.

She knew she had done the right thing. She kept telling herself that a baby would be in the way. After all the pain of the preceding year including a miscarriage, her marriage marred with conflict, her genuine although less than perfect attempt to be a mother to Heidi, the last scenario she expected was to become pregnant again. Her rocky marriage along with her insecurities of mothering a child on her own left no room for the entrance of a third participant into her tumultuous life.

Pregnant again, she had sighed. The irony was that just a year earlier, simply twelve months before her second abortion, she had rejoiced in the prospects of a new baby to round out their family.

Only the year before, she had been ready for the child that she discovered she was carrying. She remembered her happiness at the chance to try to get it all right. She was married. She was older. More secure. She and Bill were newlyweds. Everything had been so different than with Heidi. It was going to be her chance to have the family she had always dreamed of having. She felt that the pregnancy could be her redemption. She wouldn't abort this child. There would be no complications, no guilt, just the sheer, utter joy of motherhood. No worrying about whether or not her child would be born with a defect. Not worrying about her child not having a father. Not worrying about the anger of her own father. This baby would make everything right that had been wrong. She would carry it; it would be born, and she would find the natural bond that had been snatched from her in the beginning with Heidi.

But her fantasy was short-lived. A few weeks into the pregnancy, her illusion of the dream baby was shattered. She began to notice spotting. Tina frantically called her gynecologist. He wanted to see her immediately.

She rushed to the doctor's office. Certainly she wouldn't lose the baby. She imagined everything that Heidi had gone through, and Heidi had been fine. This baby she had wanted from the minute it was conceived. She never imagined she would lose her child, the baby that she had planned to conceive. But she did lose the child that she had so desperately wanted. She miscarried in the doctor's office. Tina had taken months to grieve the loss. She had suffered deeply. Forced to take Valium in order to sleep and to have a bit of calm from her intense emotions caused by the miscarriage, she had just come back to an emotional equilibrium when the news came to her again in the middle of a failing marriage that she was again expecting a baby.

So much had happened in a year. Tina no longer felt welcoming to a new child. A baby in the face of all the circumstances that she was facing. She felt almost schizophrenic. One minute she wanted a baby, the next she didn't. Heidi, she had wanted, was pushed to give up, and had her anyway. The second child she had wanted and lost. And she was pregnant again. The only thought of which she was certain was that she couldn't have a baby.

She couldn't bring a child into the marriage as insecure as their future was. Their marriage had been difficult from the beginning. They were so different the two of them. His family was formally educated. Her family had a tenacious education of common sense and hard work. Although each had been financially successful, their value systems were completely at odds. Tina and Bill had never argued very much seemingly because the passion for each other had been missing for whatever reason. They seemed to drift further apart with no commonality to bring them together. Tina wanted her marriage to work. She knew how much stress a baby would bring to her marriage, and she just couldn't bring a baby into the world. So she had made a second appointment at a second clinic, and although she had sworn she would never experience abortion again, she was lying in the same recovery room waiting for the same emotions to leave her that had racked her before.

As she was released from the clinic and walked out into the waiting room where Bill was sitting, Tina saw the same sentiment in Bill's eyes. He had agreed that a baby would only complicate their lives and relationship, but at the moment of reality, the truth seemed to overwhelm the both of them. What had once seemed to be an easy procedure that would fix their problem ended up somehow driving the wedge further between them, complicating their relationship in a way that Tina would probably never fully understand. She knew their marriage was over. She just needed a reason to leave and, shortly after her second visit to the abortion clinic, her aunt and uncle gave her a place to go.

As she drove Heidi and all their belongings up to New Jersey, she knew in her heart that her marriage would never recover. Her aunt and uncle had invited her to Elizabeth, NJ for a fresh start. Everyone saw Tina struggling. She was struggling as a young mother, a wife, a young woman who was unsure of herself. Most of all, she was struggling with confusion. She was confused about why her life had become so complicated and why her marriage had fallen apart. Her life had become characterized by a series of choices that had resulted in a myriad of confusion. All Tina knew was that she had an intense desire to create a different life from the one she was living, and she knew in her heart that her childhood home held the answer.

Chapter Thirteen

The angelic voices filled her head as her disquieting uncertainty slowly dissipated. The music sounded like heaven, or rather, the way she would have imagined heaven sounding. She had walked into Calvary Chapel feeling uneasy. Church was for the morally superior. God was for people who lived a different kind of existence than she lived. Church was the last place she would have imagined being.

Her aunt and uncle had seen her reeling from her failed marriage, drug and alcohol use, and her career that lacked promise and a future. They opened their arms to her. They wanted to see her find the answer to her unfruitful search for happiness. Tina believed that with a change of scenery, she could find a new job and maybe even a new husband. She had left South Carolina just a few days before a drug raid occurred in the apartment of one of her friends with whom she frequently partied. She knew that if she stayed in Spartanburg, she would not be the mother for Heidi that she wanted so desperately to be.

The church was one block away from the house in which she had spent her childhood in Elizabeth, NJ. The building that housed the congregation was the very building where her father had gone to grade school. Tina smiled at the irony. She had come back to her past to find her future and to make a life for her little girl. Tina smiled at Heidi. Six years old. She was a little lady. She loved wearing her little frilly dresses and shiny black leather shoes with white lace socks. She, too, was mesmerized by the music.

The choir sang of Jesus and His love. Tina wondered who Jesus was. She defined God only by one experience. God was the Being who had supposedly saved Heidi from death. All of the doctors and nurses had told her that God had delivered Heidi. There was no other explanation but a miracle at the hands of God. On a conscious level, she could never fathom God saving her child, but sitting in a church filled with people who were praising God, she began to be swept away by a sentiment she had never experienced before, and although she didn't have the answer in her logical mind, she allowed herself to be taken over by the most peaceful and joyous emotions she had ever experienced.

Song after song, her sentiments intensified. The choir continued to sing about Jesus. She saw the looks on their faces. The passion with which they sang the words. The way in which their eyes looked toward Heaven, their hands toward the sky as if they could touch this Jesus of which they sang so fervently. About His death for her. His resurrection. The peace that He gives. The pain He relieves. The promise of Heaven to those who believe. *How could this be?* And then somewhere deep within her, she knew that Jesus was real. She felt Him speak to her. Although she didn't fully understand, she felt His spirit stirring in her, allowing her to believe. She wanted to believe that what she was feeling was real. She closed her eyes and savored the rush of emotion that gave her the impression that her soul was about to experience a transformation.

The pastor stood at the pulpit to speak. Tina lingered on his every word. She wanted to know more. She had to know more. He spoke of Christ and His death. He spoke of lives restored. Of sins forgiven. He spoke of pain that could be healed. He spoke of broken spirits and how God could put lives back together when there seemed to be no hope. Tina felt as if there were a huge spotlight in the ceiling and that the pastor had dimmed the lights all around her to put the huge spotlight only on her. He spoke to her heart. He was telling the story of her very life. And she was moved. She was moved to accept the gifts that God had in store for her. She wanted for Him to change her life. She wept. She wept tears of sadness over the life she had chosen to lead, and at the same time, she cried tears of joy at the prospects of forgiveness. Forgiveness from God that would allow her to forgive herself.

Tina bowed her head, and with tears streaming from the deepest part of her soul, she asked God to forgive her. She experienced grief for her transgressions. The way she was living her life. For the empty search that had led her only further from her Heavenly Father. She was remorseful for the choices she had made. And at the same time, she was relieved of her guilt in knowing that she was forgiven. She had come to her childhood home to be reborn. To find newness in life and to discover her Heavenly Father and the peace that He had given to her in the building so close to where she had experienced her initial earthly birth.

After the benediction, Tina put her arms around her uncle.

"Uncle Gene, did you tell that pastor everything I've ever done in my life?"

"Of course not. Why?"

"It's like he was talking directly to me."

Gene smiled.

"I told him nothing."

CHAPTER FOURTEEN

The following morning, the sun was beaming, the sky a baby blue, the air brisk, and Tina's thoughts, after a lifetime of being indistinct and unclear, were focused and sure. She walked down the streets of Elizabeth. Above the small buildings of the small town emerged the skyline of New York City. No longer did it seem menacing; she had an amazing peace and security about what was in front of her and about what her future would bring to her. She felt as if a fire had started in her the morning before and was fueled by her newfound faith in what God had done. He had given her Heidi, but through a seemingly more impossible act, she had been given contentment.

She continued down the street and stopped for a moment to look in the window of the pet store, but the sound of music beckoned her to continue her stroll down the street. A man was strumming his guitar singing about Jesus. Tina stood for a moment listening to the man. His eyes closed, his head thrown back, tears rolling down his cheeks. Tina understood. She had laughed before at the men on the street corner who would ask if she knew Jesus. They were fanatics. Crazy people. They knew nothing. But finally, she understood what and why the men wanted to tell her. She knew why the man was singing so ardently about his faith. She knew the restoration that God could bring. It was as if her whole life had been a plan that had led her to that very moment. God had saved Heidi. He had allowed her to move to Elizabeth at the very moment that she was so broken she saw no hope. She had been so dejected that she needed to feel God in a miraculous way in order to believe and in order to accept the fact that He loved her. She closed her eyes and allowed the music once again to envelop her. The peace. The joy. The renewal. All the feelings that she had never imagined she could find, God had brought them to her and her to Him.

The man ended his song, opened his eyes, and smiled. "Lady, do you know Jesus Christ as your Lord and Savior?"

"Yes I do." Tina lifted her hand in the air and was filled with joy to announce her new-found faith to anyone who would listen.

A large wooden stick was attached to the homemade poster that lay on the ground. Tina timidly approached the sign, picked it up, and read. *Abortion kills.* She regretted being there most of all because of the unfamiliar twinge she experienced as she read the sign.

"What is it we're doing here again?"

"This hospital is performing abortions and we're protesting." Her friends seemed so adamant, Tina dared not ask more. She had come along with some friends from church only because they asked, and she wanted to know more. But why they were protesting, Tina was unsure. She couldn't possibly ask why they were protesting. Then she might have to tell them that she had been to the clinic twice. She herself had had two abortions. She had not had them in a hospital, but she had gone to a clinic. *What was bad about a hospital performing abortions, and why were they saying that abortion was murder?*

"Come on, Tina."

Tina picked up the sign and held it over her head. "Choose life. Abortion kills," the other protesters chanted. They were yelling, their faces red. Their anger and ardor obvious. They were, they said, trying to prevent the killing of the unborn. Tina was silent. *Abortion kills? What does that mean? And choose life?* Had she done something so terrible? And why were these people so passionate about abortion. She wanted to ask. She should have asked. She didn't dare ask. Maybe she really didn't want to know. She continued to walk around silently, the sign held just above her head. *Abortion kills.*

Tina packed up their belongings into their car, and once again as when she had left as a child, said goodbye to Elizabeth to return to South Carolina. Driving down the interstate, she felt as if she had found the newness of a child. Her life seemed to sprawl out ahead of her as the interstate led her back to a beautiful life with the peace she had found. She couldn't wait to tell Bill about how she had changed. How she would be different. How she would be a good wife and mother. No more partying, no more drugs. She knew that God wanted her to go back to her marriage, and she was determined to work out their problems. Tina looked over at Heidi. She wanted most of all to be a good mother to this little girl that God had so miraculously given her. Tina breathed a prayer to thank God for giving her a second chance. And in the back of her mind, she couldn't shake the haunting of carrying the sign, "Abortion kills."

CHAPTER FIFTEEN

Again, she was pregnant. The words had struck her. There
was disbelief that she could be pregnant again. The fear that a
baby would bring too much stress into her already fragile marriage. She was working hard so that she and Bill could stay
together. She didn't want a baby. She wasn't even sure that
they could stay together, and she had Heidi. What if the marriage didn't work and she were left with Heidi and a child on
the way? This is not how she had planned it. This is not how
she had wanted it. She needed her marriage to work, and a
baby would be in the way.

She knew she was pregnant, and she knew she didn't want
the child, but she knew that she couldn't go through the pain
of abortion again, so when she saw the signs of possible miscarriage, part of her was terrified, but part of her hoped for an easy
answer. She knew the pain of abortion. She couldn't go
through that pain again. Maybe she was miscarrying. She
drove frantically to the doctor's office.

"You have to be checked into the hospital. You could be miscarrying. We have to see what's going on."

Dr. Rubel once again. "We can either do an ultrasound to
see what's going on, or we can go ahead and do a D&C. We
would dilate the cervix and then we would use an instrument to
scrape the inside of your uterus."

"Do the D&C." The words came out automatically. She knew what she wanted, and she couldn't have a baby. She took a deep breath and waited for the anesthesia to numb her.

As she awoke, reality began to come to her. She had miscarried, she thought. Perhaps she would never know if the baby would have survived. She was sure she had been miscarrying. She had been spotting. She wasn't responsible for the miscarriage. She knew that. Moments later, however, the doctor entered the room and confirmed what she had hoped would never be verified.

"The baby was fully intact. You weren't miscarrying."

The words fell on her ears, but failed to penetrate her mind. Maybe because of shock, maybe because of guilt. She had seemingly become numb to the idea of pregnancies, children, convenience. She had not planned to abort her child. She just felt the inconvenience of its existence. The timing was all wrong. After all, the doctor should have told her there was a chance. He had, in fact, been the one to offer the choice. D&C or ultrasound. He was the professional. Had he thought there was a chance that the baby would have been intact, he would have never proposed the option. He was a doctor. They were required to protect life. To do no harm. She hadn't aborted a child. She had followed a suggestion by her gynecologist. Her medical records did not call the procedure an abortion. The doctor did not mention the word. Tina, herself, denied the word. All who were concerned denied the word. She simply elected a D&C. That's all. And the justifications continued, but the words lingered, not in her mind, but in her mother's heart, "The baby was fully intact." And as she had twice before, she shoved that part of her aside in hopes that she could forget the emotional spirit in her and focus on her own logic. "It wasn't convenient. It wasn't even an abortion."

It was over, and once again, denying her sensitivity to the idea of losing another child, she felt relief. Relieved that she wouldn't have to face a pregnancy in the prospects of a failing marriage and relieved that she wouldn't have to experience the physical pain of an abortion. She was, however, a little sad somehow, and although her rational side tried to deny this sadness, the haunting of her lost child managed to touch her somewhere. Maybe denial had set in. Or conceivably she was much too hardened by the series of events that had been her life, but somewhere among the stones of her heart was a soft spot of human clay that would stay tender and dormant until the moment arrived for its voice to be heard. And then there was the image of her and the sign and *Abortion kills* and what did it all mean? And what had she protested that day? And as she lay in the hospital after a D&C had taken her baby that had been intact, or, rather, after she had opted for the abortion that had taken her baby that would have lived had she waited to see the ultrasound, or that could have lived had she not said the words, she felt the selfishness that had become so deeply entrenched in her soul.

The doctor entered the room to discharge Tina and to be sure she was ready physically to go home. He gave her the papers for her discharge. "If you keep having these things, you'll never be able to have a baby."

In her denial, Tina wondered what he meant. These things. Was he afraid to admit what had just happened? He had not wanted to use the word abortion. Tina had wondered if his own conscience would not allow the word. He was seemingly bothered. Possibly he regretted giving her the option. Or maybe, in a way, he felt a bit responsible for the "thing". Had he not given her the choice, she would have had the ultrasound. She would have seen the baby was alive. She would have had to make the conscious choice. They would have had to use the word abortion. They would have been forced to have the conversation, the honest talk. She would have never have chosen to abort again. The pain had been too great. Or would she have? And had she chosen abortion again, would she have been able to live with herself?

The truth was, as hard as she had tried to deny it, she had chosen abortion. She had not opted for the ultrasound. She had known how difficult the decision was to abort, and she had not wanted to make the conscious decision again. She, herself, had found a way out, and although the doctor had given her the choice, she had preferred to find out after the fact if the baby had been alive than to find out before and have to make the decision with full knowledge.

She walked out of the hospital feeling the numbness that had become so common to her. She told herself and her husband that she was relieved. Relieved. So why did she feel so sad? The words bounced through her head. Relief filled her. Had she not had the D&C, she would have given birth to a child. A *baby*.

If you keep having these things, you may never be able to have another baby.

Chapter Sixteen

Tina moved her hand across her stomach as if she were actually caressing her baby. Her daughter Stephanie had been ten months old when Tina had stopped nursing her, and Tina had immediately begun taking birth control pills to prevent a pregnancy so close to her second child. She and Bill wanted another child but they wanted to wait until Stephanie was a little older. One month after Tina was forced to stop taking the pill because of the nausea it caused her, she became pregnant again. The timing was once again wrong. She had not planned to have a child so soon, but through watching Heidi grow, giving birth to Stephanie, and allowing her faith in God to lead her to the idea of life and God's desire to give children life, Tina found herself with a different perspective about carrying the child that was growing inside of her. She felt her baby kick and move inside her womb. She smiled and ran her hand once more over her stomach. At that moment, she knew. She knew that she had a life growing inside of her. For the first time in her life, she understood that she carried the most precious creature that could exist. A perfect little human being that was one in and of itself. The miracle of life that God had created inside of her finally became real and in that realization, she felt a sadness that she had taken a lifetime to learn how sacred life was, how beautiful God's creation was, and how lucky she was to be able to carry God's creation in her very own womb. She realized that God had entrusted her with a human being, and she was grateful to have the chance to learn more about God through carrying one of His miracles.

Six months pregnant, she thought. She remembered back to the little baby that had been fighting for its life in the hospital. The woman again in the clinic who had been as far along as Tina was at that moment. The baby that was living in her was a child. A living, breathing being that would be allowed to be born. The baby's life would not be cut short because of inconvenience or because it was not conceived at the right time. She was beginning to grasp the concept of life. Of choosing life rather than convenience. Of being willing to allow babies to enter into the world although it would not be in her time. She hadn't wanted a child so soon after Stephanie had been born, but she realized that through all her pregnancies before this one, she had taken control over life and the lives of the children that God had wanted to give to her. She had tried to abort Heidi, she had aborted two more children. She had tried desperately to have Stephanie, and here she was again with a pregnancy that she hadn't planned. Only this time was different. This time, she began to understand about God and His plan. God had a plan for this child she was carrying, and she understood that life is not life only because she wanted the life to be born. She had finally grasped that God wanted all life. And although the life may not have been in her plan, this life was in God's perfect plan. He needed to be born. He would be born. She somehow knew it would be a boy. Jacob would be his name, and he would be born not only because she wanted him to be born, but also because she was certain that God wanted him to be born.

Tina with her brother Michael in New Jersey on Easter Sunday at age 4.

Tina and her brothers and sister in a family photo.

Tina at the age of 20, taken at the Marriott in Atlanta.

Heidi and Steven at his prom. Heidi is now married to Steven.

Tina and Heidi in Baton Rouge, LA at one of their first speaking engagements.

Tina and Heidi in their first promotional photograph.

Tina and Heidi on a talk show in Milwaukee WI.

Tina and Heidi at a speaking engagement in California.

Tina and Heidi in Freemont Ohio.

Tina and Heidi on a talk show with another abortion survivor (Gianna Jesson) sharing her testimony.

Tina and Heidi at Focus on the Family *with Dr. Dobson, Mrs. Diana DePaul, and Gianna Jesson.* Photo: © Focus on the Family. All rights reserved. Used by permission.

Tina and Heidi with Judy Brown and a friend at a birthday party in Virginia for Mrs. Brown.

Tina, Heidi, and Stephanie at a funeral and memorial service for an "Aborted Child" in Birmingham, Alabama.

Stephanie and Jacob and, of course, Charles & Kitty (mother and son).

Tina and Jacob at a Crisis Pregnancy Center Banquet in Michigan.

At Tina and Greg's Wedding with children, son-in-law, and granddaughter

Greg playing his guitar at Tina and Greg's farm.

Tina and her new grandson, Dylan.

Tina's grand-
daughter
Mychaela.

Tina and her Arabian
mare's GL7 Arrianna
and GL7 Lyric.
Arrianna is having a
baby in April 2002.
Her first Arabian baby.

Tina's newest
Arabian mare, Audi,
is a nineteen-year-
old mare.

CHAPTER SEVENTEEN

Tina's friend Susan had invited her to a meeting of the Spartanburg Citizens for Life. All Tina knew was that Citizens for Life was an anti-abortion group. All she really knew about the pro-life movement centered around her one experience with the protesters at the hospital. She remembered their passion but had been embarrassed to ask. People who were so passionate about a cause that she didn't understand were a bit intimidating for her, and then there was the shame. The shame she was beginning to feel about her abortions. She had never thought abortion was wrong although in her heart she had realized the sadness.

She had never understood the passion for protesting against abortion. She was drawn to the idea. Perhaps through curiosity, she wanted to see for herself. She wanted to find out the source of the enthusiasm that drove the pro-life movement. She had always sensed that abortion was unnatural and sad. She had assumed that she felt a sadness only because a part of her had wanted to have those children or perhaps she had continued to feel some guilt over the events that had passed with Heidi and the botched abortion.

She accepted the invitation to the banquet. She decided to keep an open mind. She felt lured to know more. The first table that caught Tina's eye when she arrived was a table covered in brochures. She went over to the table and picked up a brochure. Before she could begin to read, she saw the picture. In the picture was a ten-week-old fetus, its arms, legs, and head ripped from its body. She could see the little baby's arms, legs, its head, its little trunk. The caption read, "A ten-week-old fetus after a suction abortion." Tina's knees became weak. Her stomach began to get that same vacant ache that she had experienced as the clinic had come into sight — the first time and the second. *That is what I almost did to Heidi. That is what I did a second time.* She couldn't finish the sentence in her head. She was dumbfounded. Stricken. And at the same time, she had to keep her composure. She had never known abortion was like that. That it tore babies apart. Limbs, head. She couldn't feel the emotions that had begun to seize her. They were much too powerful for then and there in that moment. But she was so aghast by the pictures, she was drawn to them. She felt bound to share them with everyone. She thought of her mother and father. Of her husband. Of her friends who had aborted children. Had they known? Had they known and not told her what she was doing?

The doctors had known. Had they expected her to know? Did everyone know what abortion was? She hadn't known. She had never imagined that what she had chosen for the babies inside her had been so contrary to nature. So barbaric. She wondered why no one had told her. Had she seen this picture before she had walked into the clinic, would she have been able to go through with tearing her baby apart? Would she have been able to go back to the clinic a second time? Would she have had the third abortion? She was shocked not only by the power of the suction that had ripped this baby apart, she was also mesmerized by the fact that this little creature that everyone called a fetus was a baby. It had little arms just like the little arms of her babies that she had held in her arms. It had two little legs, a little head. It had a little body. It was formed. It just needed to wait inside the womb of its mother to be nurtured and fed by her body so that it would be strong enough to face the outside world. And she had not given her babies the chance. Heidi. Heidi could have been torn apart in her womb by the suction that had seemed to consume her entire body. She truly was a miracle. Tina finally understood the miracle. The odds were that Heidi should have died. She had every chance to die, but God had held her. Protected her. Protected her from her own mother. She picked up handfuls of the brochures and slipped them in her purse. At the time, she was unsure what she would do with them. She only felt pulled to take them.

Tina had an unbridled urge to give the brochures to everyone she saw, particularly women whom she knew had aborted children. She was especially eager to see their reaction. Had they known what they had done and just hidden reality from themselves or had they been like her?

The following Saturday morning, Tina went to her hairdresser. She knew that this woman had had an abortion. She pulled the brochure out of her pocket, turned to the picture of the aborted fetus and said, "Can you believe this? This blew my mind." The woman stood motionless as she looked at the photograph. She put it over to the side. Tina thought she had said "Wow" or something similar, but, like most women, she had been living in silence for so long about what she had done, she wasn't comfortable discussing it. Tina was. She was dying to talk about abortion. To talk about her new-found knowledge about what abortion really was. She was inspired to tell the world the truth about abortion. That it wasn't an easy answer. That it wasn't painless. That it wasn't just removing a little ball of tissue. Her passion moved her to tell more people her story, and as she told more people, she felt more and more impassioned to tell the world her story—the story of her attempted abortion and her proof that abortion didn't terminate a pregnancy. It terminated a life. This realization pricked her heart, and she became more and more burdened by what she had done, and the denial became less possible as reality slowly pushed its way to the surface from her heart to her head.

CHAPTER EIGHTEEN

The following week, Tina was in the middle of her daily devotional and prayer time she had scheduled for herself every morning. Before she continued in her study of Psalms, she closed her eyes and began to meditate, but all she could see were the pictures that were so graphically displayed in the brochures she had picked up at the pro-life banquet.

She saw Heidi's face. She imagined all the sadness Heidi had experienced knowing that her own mother had not wanted her. She thought of what she had planned for Heidi and how only God could have protected her as a baby. Tina thought of the second abortion and how she had felt relief and had buried her sadness and guilt. She wondered if it had been a boy or a girl? What would he look like? What would he be as an adult? And the saddest moment of all, she saw her ultimate selfishness in her third abortion. She had not been pressured by anyone. She had been only selfish. A baby had not been what she had wanted. Her heart had been hardened by the first two abortions, so with the third, she had not even hesitated. She had felt nothing but relief that she wouldn't have to go through a pregnancy. At the same time Tina was experiencing this grief, she wanted to stop. The pain and the guilt of aborting her own children were too much for her to bear. Part of her wanted to shove those unfamiliar feelings back deep inside where they had been lying dormant all that time. And then she thought of

God. The thought that she had displeased Him disheartened her even more. But she knew about His forgiveness. All she had to do was ask.

Tina picked up her Bible, turned to Psalm 51, and began to read. The words fell upon Tina's heart as if she were saying the words herself. She felt the Psalmist's pain as he beckoned to God for mercy.

> For I acknowledge my transgressions: and my sin is ever before me, Against thee, thee only, have I sinned, and done this evil in thy sight... Behold, thou desirest truth in the inward parts: and in the hidden part thou shalt make me to know wisdom... Hide thy face from my sins, and block out all mine iniquities. Create in me a clean heart, O God; and renew a right spirit within me.

Her sin had been revealed. Tina knelt to the side of her bed stricken. She was stricken with guilt, with fear, with grief. *Forgive me, God. I have sinned against you.* The tears began to flow like a stream that had been blocked and just released. She felt as if her feelings had been pushed so far down into her being that when they resurfaced, they seemed foreign to her as if they were not really her own. She had sinned. Those babies had been a part of her, but they had been much more than that. Those babies had been lives aside from her. Creations from God that she had chosen to terminate. They had been inconvenient. At the wrong time. They had been like a bad mistake in the middle of her own wishes. And yet she knew at that moment that they were not God's mistake. He knew the time they were to be born. He knew the circumstances — although not perfect. He knew what they would be someday even if she hadn't. Tears poured from her eyes, feelings gushed from her heart. And as painful as that moment was, she was relieved that she *could* feel, for she had almost believed that she never would be able to feel again. She continued to pray. She prayed for deliverance, for healing, for God's mercy. And she received all that she had asked. She stood from her bed with a renewed heart that had been humbled through the realization of her sin

along with the calm that came to her from contrition, repentance, and the love that God had shown her by healing her
soul.

CHAPTER NINETEEN

The streets of downtown Spartanburg bustled with activity as the annual festival marking the arrival of spring brought out local merchants, street vendors, other community groups, and a plethora of people from all across the social spectrum. Tina had become an active member of the Spartanburg chapter of Citizens for Life, and the chapter took the opportunity of Spring Fling to distribute information about the pro-life movement.

The booth was covered with brochures much like the brochures that had enlightened her about what really happens during the abortion procedure. Tina flipped through the pamphlets once again. She needed to be reminded. As grotesque and graphic as the pictures were, she needed to see them to guard the passion that had ignited in her for helping to spread the truth that had somehow escaped her before. She picked up the plastic fetal models and ran her hands over them starting at the heads and feeling down to the feet of the tiny figures. She sighed at the progression of how a baby would naturally come into the world if allowed. She picked up one after the other each becoming bigger and bigger as each month passed, the little child preparing to take its first breath. As painful as the truth seemed, she had to see it. She had to face what she had done in order to make sense of her decisions and in order to save the life of some other child whose mother may be contemplating abortion.

There was the question running through her head of how she could possibly justify telling her story. How would she explain away the fact that she had experienced a miracle with Heidi? She had been blind to the idea that she had almost aborted a life. She had seen first-hand what abortion would have cost her. And yet the two other abortions. How could she possibly explain them to women who asked? She could never be dishonest. She could never simply tell the story of a scared seventeen-year-old who had felt cornered into having an abortion. "The poor child," people would say. "She had no guidance. She didn't know." That part of the story may be true, but the other part of the story would show her as being more calculating and less innocent. The additional abortions had simply been a measure of the state of her soul. They were proof of the egotism that had taken her soul hostage leaving her desensitized to the maternal instinct that would normally lead a woman to protect her offspring. She couldn't accept the pity of other people knowing that somewhere in her conscience she had been given enormous evidence to the implications of terminating a life, but she had been able to ignore her conscience, all the while burying the truth far down below the self-centeredness that had overtaken her spirit. She had sinned, and she wanted to share the whole experience of her transformation, not just the part that would evoke sympathy or understanding or at least a bit of tolerance for the ignorance of her youth. She knew she would be criticized, but she had to tell the truth. The whole truth.

Tina placed the model gently back on the table. Her thoughts were interrupted by three young girls who passed her on the street. The giggles of young girls. Innocently skipping down the street, hand in hand. Seemingly oblivious to the kind of adult behavior into which Tina had plunged herself at about their age. Tina smiled at their unsophisticated air. Just like little Stephanie.

It was so hard to believe that Stephanie was already in second grade. By Tina's memories of her own childhood, Stephanie seemed so much younger, almost baby-like in her innocence. She thought back to the week before. Tina was still seething with anger over her discussion with Stephanie's teacher. She had called Tina to come in for a conference. She was concerned about Stephanie's behavior. Tina had rushed to the school as soon as she got the call terrified that Stephanie had been behaving badly, refusing to do homework, or acting out in class. Her mind thought of the worst. Her little Stephanie who seemed so young and so innocent. What could be happening? Tina had sat down with the teacher earnestly ready to do all she could to discipline her child and to help her get back on track.

"I'm a bit worried about Stephanie."

"Why? Is she causing problems in class? Is she not doing her work? If she's disrupting class, she will certainly be punished."

"I'm concerned about Stephanie because she seems to be a bit immature for her age."

"In what way? Is she unable to do the work required of her?"

"It's not that at all. Stephanie's a bright child. She's very well behaved. It's just that she seems to be more immature than the other girls. I'm concerned most of all because she still enjoys playing with dolls." Mrs. Smith spoke in a whisper.

Tina had been momentarily too stunned to find a response. Her childhood began to race through her mind. Her losing her virginity at thirteen. Her knowing too much about her father's infidelity. Her being forced to come to grips with too much too soon. And she always swore to herself that her daughter would be a child. She would never force her daughter to be an adult at such a young age. To force her to accept information that she was too young to process maturely. She would never do that to her daughter. She knew the effects of too much too soon. Tina had been enraged. She had scarcely been able to guard her calm.

"Great! That's great news. I hope Stephanie is playing with dolls at twelve. She could be doing a lot worse."

All Tina had been able to do after her retort was get up from her chair and leave the room. She was angry and even saddened, but oddly she felt a sense of pride. Sad for the fact that so many people neglected to cherish innocence in children and proud that she was succeeding in keeping her daughter from losing her innocence too soon.

Tina had known from her own experiences what a lack of guidance could do for a young and vulnerable mind — not only from her own experiences, but also from the young women with whom she had begun working in an inner-city ministry in Spartanburg. She was able to mentor girls who were the daughters of friends with whom Tina had done drugs when she was a teenager. There were girls who came in to be counseled who were drug addicts, many of whom had several children out of wedlock. The young women had no concept of family nor of mothering children. Tina had brought them into her home and had shown them how to cook for their children. Such simple tasks as planning meals seemed enormous to them as they fell under the weight of debilitating drug and alcohol addictions. Tina had seen many girls whose lives changed immediately. Some of them had seen through Tina the importance of faith and family, but Tina was saddened by the idea that so many of them had never been taught about the importance of God and family at a much younger age.

A middle-aged woman walked by just after the girls. She looked over at the sign, stopped, and approached Tina. "I'm an ER nurse and I see case after case of abused children coming through the emergency room everyday. How could you not believe that abortion is better for a child than to be abused?"

Tina responded. "I can only speak for myself. I don't abuse my children. I'm from an upper middle class home. I take care of my children and I had abortions. Three of them. And I regret all three. Just because you don't plan a child doesn't mean you abuse it. And don't you think that abortion is the ultimate form of child abuse?"

Tina picked up a pamphlet and gave it to the woman.

"Here. This is what abortion does to children and to women."

The woman glanced down at the brochure, slipped it into her bag, and hurried away. Tina imagined that the woman would never look at the brochure again. A nurse. A woman devoted to saving life could not comprehend the taking of life in such a barbaric way. As frustrating as the thought was, she understood that she would never change everyone's mind. She had only been called to speak the truth, and if the life of one child in her own lifetime of sharing was saved from being terminated in an abortion clinic, all her work would be justified.

CHAPTER TWENTY

She recognized that she had been bothered by something, someone, or some event that day. She sat on her hotel bed. Heidi had long since been sleeping but Tina had a disheartening sensation that she couldn't shake which prevented her from sleep. *It isn't just that I'm away from home,* she thought. She was used to the disquietude of hotel room after hotel room. City after city.

Ever since *Focus on the Family* had published her story, Tina had found herself jettisoned into a demanding schedule of appearances all across the country. The editor of *Focus on the Family* magazine had heard about her story and had contacted Tina to set up an interview. She would be featured on the cover of the magazine. Tina had been elated that she would have so many people who would read her story, and, as a result, she had been certain that many lives would be changed. The editor of the magazine had come to her home, interviewed her for several days, and then Tina had waited impatiently for the edition to be released. She had known her story would touch lives, but she never knew just how many lives would receive healing because of her sharing her story with the world. She had received letters from all across the country. Letters from women who had suffered the pain of abortion. Men who couldn't forgive themselves for suggesting their girlfriends have abortions. Men who had begged for a different outcome than the termination of a pregnancy but had been given no choice. She received letters from people who were in prison. People who were minutes from committing suicide until they read about God's healing power which had saved Tina's life. Tina had been encouraged by the responses and was even more focused on getting out the message—the message of life and the message of life in God.

She had received letters from Africa, Australia, and New Zealand. She had received a letter from a woman who had been traveling on a train in Germany, picked up the magazine, read the article, and immediately penned a letter to Tina expressing to her how the story of Heidi changed her life. She had received letters from young women who had been planning to go to an abortion clinic as soon they could make an appointment, but someone had given them a copy of the magazine, and they had made the choice of life for their babies.

The magazine article had opened many doors for her ministry. She had speaking engagements scheduled for two years in advance. She was asked to give the testimony of her transformed life all over the nation. And at the same time, the pro-life movement was injected with a renewed fervor. The renewal began in the early 1990s in California with the controversial rescues which were occurring in many abortion clinics. Groups began to schedule sit-ins in front of abortion clinics. Sidewalk counselors would line the streets to try to stop women from going into the clinic. The anti-abortion groups wanted to be sure that the women were informed. They wanted to make sure that the women were certain of the possible physical ramifications of abortion as well as the psychological ones.

Everywhere the pro-lifers congregated, the pro-abortionists were there also. They were trying to defend their cause. Their shout was "the woman's right to choose." They saw abortion as a choice. The ultimate choice of the woman was to decide what went on inside her body. The pro-lifers took the stance that the baby inside the woman's body was not the woman's body but a living entity in and of itself. The debates were heated and the passions were magnified.

The revival of the movement coupled with the feature in *Focus on the Family* had opened doors for Tina that she never imagined would be opened. It was like her life had been prepared for that particular period of renewal. God had prepared her in her heart at the right moment, and she was in the middle of this awakening. People were not only being awakened to the idea of life but they were also being awakened to the idea that men and women were not responsible for creating life — God was. And in the same moment that people were recognizing their limitations in the grand scheme of life, they were pouring out their praise to God who does have the ultimate power in creating life.

On the other side of this spiritual awakening was the pro-abortion movement. Tina saw them as people driven not by passion but by anger, some even by rage. Their driving emotion seemed to be anger and resentment. Tina wasn't sure why they would be angry because they had the law on their side. They had fought hard to allow abortion to be legal, and they were still angry. They were angry that she called a fetus a living human being and angry that she allowed her daughter to be the living proof.

This idea had been most evident that day. She and Heidi had traveled to Buffalo, New York. Tina had been asked to speak at the Spring of Life Rally that had drawn many supporters of the pro-life movement, but had also attracted many abortion proponents as well. The usual radical pro-abortion groups were on hand. The crowds were enormous. Tina and Heidi were trying to work their way through the crowd perhaps to counsel someone who was hurting maybe even someone who was on the opposite side of the debate. The streets were so mobbed, the crowd so angry, they were unable to get through. Tina was frightened. She could see the anger and the hostility. She knew that they were in a dangerous environment. One that was not welcoming to her and her daughter. She had an overwhelming fear and tentativeness as she tried to slip through the crowd of people. She was unsure what was ahead of her and was apprehensive about what step to take next.

Women were screaming about their right to choose. "Tell them the truth," Tina said. She felt herself beginning to shout. She contained her zealousness for she knew that she had to reach these people, and if she began to shout, they would only try to shout louder. "Give these women a choice if you are pro-choice. When they come into the clinic tell them, ' You can become sterile from a botched abortion. You can die from a legal abortion. You could have symptoms of post-abortion syndrome for the rest of your life.' You don't give them a choice. You give them abortion. Tell them the truth. Tell them that they will regret their decision for the rest of their lives. Tell them that if they decide to abort their babies there is the possibility they will never become pregnant again. Tell them that there isn't a 'fetus' in their womb. Call it what it is. A baby. Their baby. Their child. Tell them." And then she began again to try to get through the crowd to go where she was scheduled to speak. Penetrating through the masses of people had been an impossibility.

As she sat on the hotel bed that night, she began to wonder what she was doing caught in the center of such controversy. She felt haunted after the events of the day. What could have haunted her so much? What had made such an impression on her? What could have possibly caused such an important abstract fear inside of her? The anxiety of desiring to go back home. To head back on the first plane to Spartanburg. To rediscover the safety of her home. Her surroundings. The comfort that gave her the ability to give the impossible. To share the seemingly unsharable. What had made her emotions so much more tender this time? There had always been a discomfort. She tried to rationalize her uneasiness. *Who would ever want to admit that they had three abortions? To anyone. Let alone thousands of people.* Those thousands of people. Many of whom had an enormous amount of respect for what she was trying to accomplish. Many of whom were so anti-abortion they couldn't fathom a way of forgiving her although she had made peace with herself and God. She was accustomed to the opinions and judgments of people. She began to shiver as the realization of what had just taken place on the streets of Buffalo began to unfold into her conscious mind.

The people. Some of the people. They were praying prayers. But not to God. They were prayers of witchcraft. Evil prayers. Prayers that were frightening. Her skin crawled as she thought of the prayers. The prayers that were being offered to gods, to evil, to stop her. To stop Heidi. She was unafraid of the prayers themselves. Her fear was more isolated than that. To be pro-choice and to fight for abortion was in and of itself in the least incomprehensible to her. But she saw many of those people as at least reasonable. She had been able to reach some of those on the side of abortion if only to give her argument. To tell them the truth. The truth that their passion for such a reprehensible activity such as abortion was not about a woman's right. It was about saving women from themselves before they made catastrophic decisions. Catastrophic for them and for society. It wasn't those people. Many in the pro-abortion movement would listen and were even flexible enough that she herself had seen pro-abortion activists change sides after hearing the truth — the truth that very few women who had experienced abortion were courageous enough to share.

Today had been different. Different in a terrifying way. Different because Tina hadn't been confronted by people. She hadn't been physically assaulted. She had been spiritually intimidated. People had summoned up their passions for abortion by using an evil premise through their demonic religion. Tina realized that her fear came mostly because she was commissioned in her heart to minister to all people. Not just those to whom serving came easily but to all people. Even those who had brought her terror. Terror in the fervency of their religion. Religion. She was uncomfortable even calling their beliefs religion, but they were entrenched in a sort of witchcraft that was completely foreign and was in Tina's mind, impenetrable and impossible to fight against. That thought was what instilled the fear in her.

The fear was even more magnified by the woman whom she had never seen and with whom she had never spoken. With whom, she felt comfortable in an odd way and fearful in another. In Tina's mind the woman had appeared to her as an angelic presence. She had comforted Tina in her confusion. She had led her when Tina was so mesmerized by the crowds that she had been unsure of why. Tina had been frustrated and afraid. She had been on the verge of giving up when the woman had approached her and had taken her by the hand. "God has led me to you to be your guide while you are here in Buffalo. Follow me."

Although the prospects of having a guide were comforting to Tina, the woman was frightening to Tina as well, for she was certain that the woman had been sent to her by God to guide her. Reassurance soothed her fear and at the same time intensified it. Her apprehension was intensified because she needed to have that woman sent to her. To help her through the unknown. The unknown that she had always imagined she had experienced. She had seen more that she thought she should have. But today. Today was different. She was out of her element and realized that her own strength, her own tenacity, and her own independence was not enough. Today she had been stripped of all the strength that she had needed to minister to others. She had been vulnerable and afraid. And she realized that she was powerless except for her faith in God. Her prayers began. They began for those who were confused about the truth of abortion and about those who had instilled such fear in her. She prayed for those who used the abortion issue for an even more sinister cause than that of abortion. They were using death as a means of sacrifice to their gods. The thought made Tina shudder. She could only close her eyes. Close her eyes and pray for strength against forces toward which she had no control.

CHAPTER TWENTY-ONE

Baby Jacob was his name. Tina wasn't sure who had named him. She thought of her own little Jacob, the little Jacob that she hadn't planned to conceive. The little Jacob who had become a part of her heart. The Jacob whom she could never imagine life without. Jacob. She repeated the name over and over in her mind.

She had had innumerable speaking engagements. She had learned somehow to deal with the struggle that she faced each time. She hadn't expected to have her wounds from the past ripped open that day. She had expected to change minds. Instead she found a memory that would stay in her mind forever as a constant reminder that she had a mission. She was called. At this assembly, she would feel the passion renewed inside of her to speak the truth.

Tina and Heidi walked up to the church. Hundreds of people filled the Epiphany Church that day. Hundreds of people had come to pay their respects to the baby who had been found by a nurse, dead in a trash can outside the hospital. Members of the press surrounded the church snapping photos. Tina and Heidi walked into the church and were escorted to their seats. At the front of the church was a little open white casket. People were walking down to the casket placing roses onto the little white box. They were weeping, staring at this little orphaned baby who had been left in a trash bin next to irreparably soiled

linens and other items of waste that had been discarded.   The
members of the media were snapping photos and filming the
baby lying in the casket. A baby whose birth should have been
rejoiced. A baby who should have been wrapped in a little blue
fleece blanket and cuddled in the arms of his mother was
instead found dead in the trash outside of an institution built to
heal the human body. Tina shook her head. She had no words
to comfort Heidi. She couldn't explain why or how. She felt
her own guilt renewed by this scene. The scene of a baby
aborted at seven months gestation, dumped into a trash can,
left among refuse. How could she explain that to her daughter,
a fifteen-year-old who had yet to experience life?

Tina could barely stand the mourning in her heart. She was
mourning her own abortions by mourning this baby who she
could see in front of her. Her abortions had been out of sight,
out of mind. She had repented. She had known that she had
done wrong, but something was aroused in her that day. It was
the intensity not of sinning, but a moment of grieving as if this
day, it seemed she were laying to rest her own children.

Tina barely heard the speaker call her name. She only heard
Heidi's as Heidi stood to go to the front to speak. She directed
Heidi to the casket. Tina stood over Baby Jacob weeping. He
was fully formed. He had two arms, two legs, ten fingers, ten
toes. Tina counted them all. His little bald head lay on the
white silk pillow, his eyes closed peacefully. A contrast to the
way he died. The burns were still on his body from the saline.
Tina imagined what he must have gone through. Feeling safe
in the womb of his mother, kicking, perhaps sucking his thumb,
rocked and calmed by the movements and voice of his mother.
Suddenly betrayal was evidenced by the saline solution that
filled his comfortable home inside his mother's womb, his safe
haven where he would have grown until strong enough to
emerge into the world. The saline was injected all around him.
His lungs burned from breathing in the foreign caustic substance. His insides must have seemed on fire as he was charred
by the solution with which his mother betrayed him. Tina

didn't care *why* the woman had chosen to abort this baby. He looked so perfect. She imagined how she had felt when her three children had come out of the womb. How perfect and soft and miraculous they had been. And here was Jacob. A baby. She had forgotten. Forgotten that these were babies that she had tried to abort and had aborted. Babies like Jacob. Baby Jacob. Her tears flowed dropping onto the casket.

Tina walked to the front of the church and climbed the steps, Heidi right behind her. Tina saw young women on the front row weeping uncontrollably. She knew their tears. She knew that they, too, had experienced abortion. She knew that they, too, must have been experiencing the reality of what abortion really is.

Tina could barely speak, and Heidi saw that she needed to speak for her mother. "That could be me lying in that casket." The words plunged into Tina's soul.

"She's right. It could have been my Heidi lying in that casket. She was one second away from death. One second from being the little baby lying in that casket. I would love to pick up this baby and tell him how sorry I am that this has happened to him. And the saddest part is that there is a woman in Detroit, Michigan who doesn't know that we are here burying her baby today. Perhaps if we could all see Baby Jacob. If we could all hold him and touch him, then we would be reminded of what abortion really is.

"As hard as this one moment is for us today, we must be thankful that God does not force us to see this event more often. He sees many babies die from abortion everyday. Imagine how He must weep over these babies He sees killed day after day.

Yes, it could have been Heidi. Instead, it is Jacob."

CHAPTER TWENTY-TWO

The green room was filled with African Americans praying fervently, their hands placed on a woman. The woman had a confidence about her. She had an air of certainty about her that made Tina somehow feel more nervous about going on the show.

Tina had appeared on several popular secular shows. She knew that her appearances were frowned upon by many in the religious community who had been the backbone of the pro-life movement. She felt that her mission had to extend to all facets of the population, even the secular world. She wanted her message to be heard by all people, and maybe in telling the message that she had experienced about life to all categories of society, not only could she save a child, but possibly her message would reach and change the hearts of many adults. She was ridiculed by many people for her appearances particularly on one talk show which was known for its questionable topics and lewd language.

Tina had been torn about appearing, but in the end her desire to reach as many people as possible won out over public opinion, and, on that very show, she was able to minister to a young girl sitting in the front row of the audience who had cried through the entire show over guilt from a pregnancy that she had terminated a few months earlier. Tina received letters from around the country after appearing on that show, letters from people whose lives had been touched by watching the program, people who would have probably not been reached any other way. Tina accepted the criticism from a few to help give the message of life to people who would not hear the miracle otherwise.

She had seen the effects of open media bias on all of the national secular programs on which she and Heidi had been featured. She had seen people turned away as audience members because of their conservative positions on abortion. She had seen audiences that were stacked to add to the hostility against her, the producers hoping to make a more "lively" show. She had been denied the opportunity to tell the whole story because of the obvious pro-abortion slant of the national media.

That day, Tina felt particularly intimidated. The show was hosted by an open advocate of abortion, and the network was widely known for its liberal positions. The positive spin was that she and Heidi had the ultimate weapon because Heidi was living and walking proof that abortion did take life, and the show would be an opportunity to give the proof to millions of people.

Tina and Heidi were taken to their places on the stage. The stage was positioned in front of the audience. There were chairs set up across the stage, and Tina was anxious to know who else would appear on the show. She was particularly curious about the woman who had had so much support with her in the green room. Their seats were just next to the woman and on the other side of her were two other women. The people in the audience were talking softly looking up at the stage waiting for the show to begin.

Finally, the show did begin. The host of the show entered the room. Loud applause, and then Tina, preparing her words in her mind, barely heard what was said until the woman from the green room was introduced as an evangelist and was asked for her opening comment.

"Do you know what abortion is?"

She took a noose she had hidden under her chair and placed it around her neck as she held onto the end of the rope above her head with her right hand.

"This is what abortion is." Some people in the audience booed, some clapped, some gasped. Tina understood this woman. The woman had known that she had been on the wrong side of the issue for the producers of the show. She had realized that she would get only a few minutes to speak. She had to make it memorable.

"Cut to a commercial."

The producers were frantic. They ran to the woman and snatched the noose from her. After the commercial break, the host introduced the next guest on the show. She was a woman in her forties, the wife of an attorney who had decided that at her age, she was too old to have a baby. The producers of the show had taken her to the abortion clinic on the morning of the show, paid for her abortion, and then brought her to the stage to tell the world how easy an abortion was. The woman was groggy, obviously sedated from the abortion procedure. She spoke slowly, her eyes only half-opened. She described the abortion in detail. She was matter-of-fact. She talked about the facility of an abortion. The ease with which she had come to the decision. Tina wanted to speak to tell the woman how sorry she was for her that perhaps in a sedated state, she felt a certain calm, but as time wore on, that calm would disappear and one day she would have to face the consequences of her decision. But Tina wasn't given the chance. The woman who had had the abortion as well as the president of a well-known women's organization monopolized the conversation, the show being obviously slanted on the side of the pro-abortion movement. When Tina's turn came to speak, she was given only a few minutes before the commercial break, and Heidi not a second. Tina thought she knew why. Heidi was proof. She was proof that abortion was the termination of a life. Then the woman who had aborted her baby that morning as well as the supporters of abortion would have to face the truth about the cause for which they were so passionate.

Tina and Heidi walked out of the studio into noisy Manhattan and walked toward their hotel. "Why?" Tina said to Heidi. "Why would they bring us all the way here to tell our story and then not allow us to talk? Why would they not want to hear our side? Our truth? Nothing has come of this trip. It was a total waste of time."

Tina and Heidi were scheduled to leave New York that afternoon but on entering their hotel room, Tina received a call from the speakers' bureau who handled her scheduling. She was asked to attend a press conference in front of one of the largest abortion clinics in Manhattan. The clinic had been scrutinized in the press for performing several botched abortions. Some women had become infected and even sterile from having abortions in the clinic. Tina felt reassured that perhaps the trip hadn't been made for the television show but for the opportunity to attend the news conference outside the clinic. She scribbled down the directions, and she and Heidi raced to get to the clinic.

Standing in front of the abortion clinic was a doctor in a white coat just beside a uniformed police officer. He stood in front of a podium. There were flashes from the photographers and microphones shoved in his face. He had just finished speaking when Tina and Heidi arrived.

"Hello, sir. This is my daughter, Heidi. She survived a botched abortion."

Tina had yet to complete her sentence when the doctor turned quickly to go into the clinic without a word, without a gesture. Nothing. He just paled as if the young lady who stood before him was a forgotten dreaded ghost of his past.

CHAPTER TWENTY-THREE

Tina had never imagined how much seeing the clinic again would bring back the memory of her abortions. Not just the pain of the abortion at the time but the emotion of knowing now what she had hidden from herself then. The other women had known and felt what had happened as well. She thought of all their tears, her own tears. She had known that something had been wrong. Something had been so unnatural about the procedure. Her body had felt the normal elements of what nature allowed to happen to her body as it prepared to carry her child. Everything about a woman would prepare her to have a child. The hormones, the maternal instinct began immediately, the feeling of a mother toward her child. Her flesh and blood. And to go against the body that was prepared to give birth, preparing itself to nourish its offspring through nine months in the womb and then continue to nourish it throughout its infancy. The body would connect with a woman's spirit to prepare her to be a mother. And to strip all these natural progressions away with a powerful suction and a tube, and collect the miracle of life and motherhood in a cup. She wanted to run into the clinic and scream her knowledge to the women before the same anomaly happened to them. Before they cried without knowing why. Before they became like the women who called her seeing aborted babies floating in a sea or would dream about hearing their aborted babies call to them, and they were unable to get to them.

Although the idea that she was telling her story freed her in
many ways, she still had moments of complete sadness, almost
grief. The guilt no longer there, but a natural sadness that she
knew would last a lifetime. The tears that would come each
time she held a baby. Her abortions were no longer her deep,
dark, black secrets. She was soothed by the idea that the truth
was being told. She knew the truth. She had lived the truth
three times. She lived constantly with the truth. The guilt had
eased when she had begun to forgive herself and to accept forgiveness from God, but the regret of what she had done stayed
with her. She judged herself harshly. She judged herself more
harshly since she had begun her ministry cognizant of the fact
that her example in the way she led her life had a great impact
on many young women and she never wanted to betray her testimony by living an immoral life. She went over her life with a
fine-toothed comb. She wanted the regret. It had somehow
humbled her. Self-righteousness could never find its way into
her soul because she always had her sorrow in the back of her
mind. In many ways, she had learned to intertwine her peace
of mind along with her grief over her past, and why her life had
taken the path it had, somehow made more sense as she told
her story, as she saved lives, and gave hope.

But watching the women come in and out of the clinic, she
was saddened that very few of the women would find their way
out as she had. Tina imagined that many of the women would
survive as if nothing had happened. They would, as she had,
push it so far down that they would never think of it consciously again, but they would have a permanent sadness that would-
n't go away until they dealt with what they had done. And
even then, they would have to learn to live with the sadness
because the act in which they were engaging in that clinic was
permanent. Permanent for the babies who were dying and permanent for the women whose bodies, minds, and souls would
cry out for the children who were so unnaturally removed from
their bodies.

Tina stood against the fence watching. Watching again the men waiting in the cars, in the parking lot. Waiting. Some of them escorting the women into the clinic. Tina searched the parking lot imagining that perhaps she could find one woman who would listen one last time before she walked into the clinic and walked out a different woman than when she had gone in. Tina wanted to scream, *Don't go in. You will never be the same. You will have emotional wounds and even if those wounds heal, the scars will always be there.*

Tina saw a young couple walking toward the door of the clinic. The man was holding the woman in his arms guiding her gently toward the entrance. She was crying.

Tina pleaded, "Don't take her in there. This will be the biggest mistake she will ever make. Don't do this to her. Don't let her do this."

Tina recognized the look in the woman's eyes. She had felt the same way. Like a mouse trapped in the corner with no way to escape. Trying to please everyone around her while something inside of her was begging her to stop. Tina could tell that this was not what she wanted. The woman was crying. The man looked at Tina, held the woman closer to him, and nudged her quickly to the door. Tina felt her heart enter the door with the woman. She prayed for strength for this woman because she knew that the moment she stepped out the door, she would never be completely at peace again.

CHAPTER TWENTY FOUR

It was a beautiful spring day in Birmingham, Alabama. By all accounts, they were surrounded by the signs of the time of year that epitomizes new life. The trees were budding again. The flowers were blooming. The birds were all perched high once again atop their houses in the trees waiting for their eggs to hatch or helping their little babies to learn to fly from the nest. Juxtaposed against the beauty of nature, the nourishing disposition of the birds, the renewing of the seasons, and the tenderness of creation lay yet another little white casket cloaked in little pastel-colored flowers and surrounded by throngs of people. Buried by those who never knew him and those he never knew.

The memorial service was held on the street. In the casket lay a baby, or rather, the remains of what had been a baby. Once again a child who had been unwelcome in the world. It was not a nation who grieved the death of this child. Only a crowd of people who wanted to see him with a proper burial and to see his body saved from being discarded. The casket held the contents of a being who had once been alive. A baby conceived, yet unwanted, uninvited, and in the end, denied life. The casket was closed due to the graphic and violent nature of the baby's death. The baby whose death had occurred on the abortion table. Its body too maimed to allow the opening of the casket because of the power of the suction machine.

Tina understood why the casket was closed. She had seen the pictures. She wondered silently if the baby had suffered. Had he felt this happening? Was he able to feel the pain?

And simultaneously with her extreme sadness, she felt anger. She felt angry that so many people were so numb to these babies. They were living, breathing human beings. And there were so many who were so angry that she was trying to keep another baby from being taken from the world prematurely. She could still hear the anger in the woman's voice on the local radio interview she had had that morning. The woman who had called to curse her for trying to save babies and for trying to spare other women the agony of having to look at a little white casket and to imagine how that the choices she had made had been so wrong. A tragedy. A barbaric tragedy for the baby and for the mother. She wondered from where the woman's anger came. The right to choose. The woman's body.

She had become used to the debate, but the anger, she knew she would never be able to understand. Wherever the pro-life movement showed up, the pro-abortion group was right behind them inciting their members to action to protect the right to choose. What had always amazed Tina was the hatred that filled their faces. They had this sense that their movement was the compassionate one. They were the ones who had the best for women in mind. They would scream to Tina and other pro-lifers the words: intolerant, haters, judges, and much worse. They were angry, and Tina was unsure why.

The anger seemed to be at its peak. Just a few weeks earlier, Tina and Heidi had been asked to attend another rally. Heidi was with her friend Gianna who was also a survivor of abortion. They were standing hand in hand singing "Amazing Grace" when a woman came to them, her face bursting with hate. She screamed, "You should have died. I wish you had died." Tina looked down at Heidi's face as she felt the pain and shock of what this woman had said. *You should have died.* Heidi and Gianna had simply continued singing, but Tina knew what the words must have done.

Tina wondered where the woman was who had entered the clinic in Birmingham, Alabama. She knew the woman had no idea that her baby's body was there in the casket waiting to be buried by strangers. The woman didn't know they were burying her baby. What would she do if she knew? Would she be angry? Would she grieve? Would she realize that she had chosen to take the life of her baby? But the woman would never know. She would never know that strangers were standing over the casket of her baby shedding tears and grieving the loss of a small human being.

CHAPTER TWENTY FIVE

Tina was asked to speak at Westside Baptist Church in Spartanburg, SC. She stood in the pulpit, looked out at the congregation, and smiled to fifteen-year-old Heidi. Once again she would pull out their story, the story she forced herself to tell. The story she hoped would save a life or restore another.

Tina spoke. "Every Sunday, my mother would dress her little granddaughter in a brand new dress, and every Sunday little Heidi would rush to put on her new Sunday dress and run out to meet the bus. The bus would come around faithfully to load up all the children in the apartment complex and carry them off to Sunday School. Heidi couldn't wait to take her seat on the bus, and if she happened to oversleep and miss the bus, Grandma was forced to drive her herself because Heidi would sob if she thought she would miss Sunday School. She loved church. She loved riding the bus. She loved learning.

"The name written on the side of the bus was Westside Baptist Church. Your bus ministry reached my daughter until we moved when she was six years old. For three years, your congregation picked up a little girl in some apartment complex who almost died in an abortion attempt. Your church faithfully ministered to a little girl who had never heard about Christ. She was surrounded by people who didn't know God, and your church opened your arms to her. Thank you. Thank you for reaching out. Churches never know what kind of lives they are touching, but you touched Heidi's life, and I thank you."

The members of the congregation wept. Many of them had remembered Heidi as a child. They had not seen her in years. None of them knew what she had survived. No one knew that she would be such a force in ministering to people all over the world. None of them had known that they were the only way she would have ever heard about God as a child. There were no dry eyes in the congregation on that Sunday morning, for they realized that they had seen a need, had made a way to fulfill it, and at the same time had touched the life of a little girl who was a walking, breathing testimony for life.

CHAPTER TWENTY-SIX

Tina opened the envelope to find a photograph of a small white cross with the words written in black: "Lisa Marie. My baby was aborted." Tina read the note enclosed with the photo to find that the cross had been found in a cemetery.

Tina had named her babies, too. She imagined how the cross served as a monument, and the moment the woman had placed the cross in the cemetery had served as part of her healing. There would be peace in forgiveness, in grieving, in actually giving her child a name. This woman had perhaps come to terms with the idea that she would never be able to go back to that day in the clinic or the hospital, to that moment when the suction began or the saline was injected or the scalpel was stuck into the baby's head to remove the contents of its skull. No matter what had happened that day, no one, no matter how regretful would be able to change it. In order to survive, the woman would have to forgive herself and finally say goodbye to the child who had never been born but had once lived within her. This woman had said goodbye. Tina had imagined a woman kneeling in the graveyard, placing her makeshift tombstone in the ground. Probably alone, most likely as she had been on the day of the abortion. She probably had placed the marker into the ground. Stood and wept. Said a prayer. Probably something like, "God, I ask your forgiveness for the sin that I committed. Please give me grace to bear the grief and

please erase the guilt from my soul. In your name I pray.
Amen." She probably knelt, looked once again at the tombstone, rose, turned around to leave, then was drawn back to the
marker for one last plea to her God. "Please take care of Lisa
Marie. Hold her in Your arms and give her all the love that her
little heart needs and deserves. Forgive me that I wasn't the one
to give it to her. Amen." Tears probably streamed down her
face. She probably stood there alone for minutes maybe hours
and then she turned to leave. She would surely guard this
moment in her heart as long as she lived, for this would be the
moment she would let go. It would be forever etched in her
memory as the moment she had let go of her guilt and her long-
ing for her child, but somehow the strain would always be
there.

CHAPTER TWENTY-SEVEN

Tina reenacted the events of the prior evening in her mind. She had a sense that she had reached several young women at the rally the night before. She thought of the peculiar meeting she had had with the man. She had felt someone approach her from behind. He had said nothing to her. Tina turned when she felt him put his hands on her shoulders. It was an elderly man. A man she had never seen. He began to pray. Tina could scarcely hear him. She recognized only a word here and there. He was asking God to bless her, to hold, and keep her. He left as quickly and as mysteriously as he had come. Tina turned to ask why he felt he should pray with her, but he had disappeared among the crowd. Tina had stood on her tiptoes, straining her neck to find him. But he was gone. He had left her with a strange feeling. She had looked for him the rest of the evening but had never found him.

As she pulled into the driveway, she had the suspicion that she had needed his prayer. Her marriage had survived many turbulent periods, but lately she found that the marriage was suffering in a way that she had not wished to admit to herself.

Tina looked around the house. It was quiet. She knew Bill was home. His car was in the driveway. She went into their bedroom, and he was in bed. Tina had suspected that he had been having an affair, so seeing him in bed at 4 o'clock in the afternoon only aroused her curiosity. "What are you doing in bed?"

"I had to work late last night."

Tina said nothing. As much as she wanted to believe him, she couldn't. She couldn't stop thinking that something was terribly wrong. She knew he was hiding something from her.

She immediately went out to his truck. On the seat was a piece of paper. On the paper was a female's name in the handwriting of what had to be a woman's, along with a local phone number. Her name was Tina. She couldn't move. She just kept staring at the piece of paper as if it held some sort of answer as to how or why this could possibly be happening to her. After several minutes, she calmed herself enough to go inside. She couldn't face Bill yet. She had to hear the news from this woman, Tina. Every time her own name ran through her mind, her knees became weak and the shock resurfaced.

"Hello?"

"Tina?"

"Yes."

"Do you know a guy named Bill?"

"Yeah. I met him at a club last Friday. Why?"

"I just need to know how you know him." Every word tortured her, but she had to know.

"I met him last Friday night in a club, and we slept together."

"Have you seem him since?"

"Yeah. We were together last night. Why? Who is this?"

"His wife. Tina, can I come over and talk to you?"

The woman on the other line was silent for a moment before she let out a timid, muffled "yes."

Tina put the receiver down and immediately ran into their bedroom to confront Bill.

"I just talked to Tina."

"Who?"

"Tina. You know. The one you met in the club last Friday night? The woman you were with last night?"

"How did you find out?"

"How could you sleep with a woman after meeting her for the first time? How could you do this to your family?"

"I love her."

"What?"

"I'm in love with her."

"Let me get this straight. You meet a woman in a club, you sleep with her the first time you meet her, and now you tell me that you're in love with her?"

Tina didn't need a response. She ran out the door and jumped into her car. She began to cry. Why was this happening? She had given her life to helping women. She had wanted to prevent other girls from traveling the road she had. She had wanted desperately to save babies and to help women heal who had already chosen abortion. She had opened the deepest parts of her soul to people she didn't even know. She had sacrificed her privacy. She had revealed her deepest secrets. And all for what? She was losing her husband. She was losing her family. She wasn't sure that any of the benefits were worth the cost.

She arrived in front of Tina's house. She sat in the car for a moment waiting. Wondering if she should. She had no other choice. She had to save her marriage for the children.

"I'm Bill's wife."

"What?"

"I'm Bill's wife. You know. The man you've been sleeping with."

The woman who was destroying her family was speechless. She motioned for Tina to come in.

"Do you know what you're doing? Do you have any idea why I was out of town? Do you realize what kind of calling is on this family? We are called to save babies, to help women. To stop abortion. To stop the pain that it causes. The pain it causes to women and the pain it causes to families, and you're destroying my family. Do you realize what you're doing?"

The woman looked down, and when she finally began to speak it was in a broken voice. She began to tell Tina about how much shame she felt. How her life had not gone the way she had planned. She knew the pain of abortion first hand. She had aborted a child as well.

Tina found a place to put her anger aside. If ever she had found a moment to test her desire to heed the calling that was on her life, the test had certainly arrived. Tina began to minister to the woman. She told her that promiscuity and bars would never give her peace. She told her of the peace that she had discovered in God and the forgiveness that she had found in being His child. And she left sure that after their meeting, the woman would end her relationship with Bill, she still wondered if their marriage could endure the betrayal.

CHAPTER TWENTY-EIGHT

It seemed that she was always waiting for him. Waiting for him to come home, to call just to tell her he would be late. Every time the phone rang, she thought it would be him telling her he was working late. But the call never came. She awoke throughout the night with thoughts of where he could be and with whom. She altered between anger and despair, fear and outrage. Drifting in and out of sleep, she waited. She thought of all the things she could have done differently. She had tried to keep her ministry in second place, her family first. She had traveled only on weekends. She hadn't taken any bookings in the summer or during the kids' Christmas vacation. Had she traveled too much? Had she not been there enough for him?

The kids. How would she tell the kids? She had tried to protect them. She had hidden so much from them. She hadn't told them the truth about why their father had not been coming home. She had held her tears so that they wouldn't know. She had to make this marriage work for them. She knew it and Bill knew it. She had to put the children first.

But as the night grew longer and she was still alone, she realized that she could no longer live with the lies. The not knowing. She could no longer handle the agony of knowing he was with someone else. Wondering when he would be home, if he would even come home at all. Where he would be sleeping.

She couldn't. As much as she wanted to protect her children, she couldn't make their marriage work alone.

As the sun came up, she awoke to find he had not come home. And this time was the last. She knew that this time, it was over. The longer she waited for him, the more determined she became.

Tina picked up the phone to call her mother and father-in-law. As soon as she heard Jane's voice she said, "It's over. I can't live this way." Jane had barely responded. She had known. Their friends had known. Everyone had known that it was just a matter of time before Tina would be forced to end their relationship.

The clocked ticked by, and with every minute that passed, she knew more and more that her marriage was over. 11 o'clock. She heard his truck pull into the driveway. She and Stephanie were in the kitchen waiting together.

"Get your things and get out."

He seemed strangely calm. "You're right, Tina. It is time. I'm not willing to take the same direction as you are. If I stay with you, I'll ruin your life. I don't want to have a family anymore, and I don't want to be married anymore."

CHAPTER TWENTY-NINE

Tina lay in bed with tears running down her face. She wanted to believe him that he was the one that God wanted her to marry. He had said the words. "God told me to marry you." And how was he so sure? She had just met him. She was confused. Confused because she was fearful of being alone but even more fearful of making a huge mistake and ending up spending her life with the wrong man.

An elderly woman who had gone to her church had invited her and the children into her home until Tina could get back on her feet. She had done nothing but public speaking for many years, and the prospects of finding a new job seemed daunting. She had come across a job at a manufactured homes dealership in Easley, finally had made enough money to get on her feet, and she and her children had moved into an apartment.

She was starting to regain some of the confidence she had lost going through the divorce. She was beginning to lose her feelings of rejection and unworthiness, and the more confident she became, the less comfortable she was in being single. Although her confidence grew in her ability to take care of herself and her children, she felt vulnerable being single. She had been married for sixteen years. She had had to learn to date again. To fight against men who had seemingly been strong Christian men who would tell her, "God told me that you were the woman I'm supposed to spend the rest of my life with." As lonely as Tina felt, and as insecure as being alone made her feel, she had to be careful before she became involved with someone. Not only did she have an obligation to her children to choose the right mate, she didn't want to live the same life that she had experienced with Bill. The other women, the estrangement, the instability, and the pain of being told by her husband that he no longer wanted her. She had to wait.

She looked over on her nightstand at a picture of her children. Stephanie and Jacob were still very much dependent on her. They had been through so much. Stephanie had been standing beside Tina the day her father had said he didn't want a family anymore. But for some reason, she looked up to him and loved him to the point of placing him on a pedestal. Tina hadn't told her the truth, and she wasn't sure that she ever would although Stephanie blamed her, she was certain. Stephanie had heard only the words from Tina for her father to leave. She had not wanted to hear the rest, and Tina would never remind her or tell her of the pain she had suffered. She would protect her daughter from the truth so that Stephanie could maintain her love and respect for her father. Tina knew how necessary the relationship was between a father and his children, and she intended to nurture that relationship for Stephanie and Jacob's sake.

Tina felt a certain comfort in her own place. The place she was able to provide for her children. Their home. But in the midst of her comfort, she was empty. She felt lonely. She needed someone. She disliked dating. She had seen many men who simply wanted to take advantage of her vulnerability. She was confused by the idea that they could use God to confuse her further.

She was still experiencing feelings of anger. She had hesitantly given up her ministry. She was angry that God would allow this to happen to her. She had sacrificed so much for Him. Her story was a hard one to tell. She had never been proud of the fact that she had had three abortions. She felt

shame and despair every time she told her story. She had continued out of obedience to God. Her family was destroyed
because of it. And then who would want her to speak when
they found out she had been divorced? They would all blame
her. Everyone would say that she had sacrificed her marriage
for the ministry. She would still go to church and raise her
children to believe in God, but she would never sacrifice so
much again. She vowed to herself to never speak again.

Her emotions swung on a pendulum between being angry at
her ministry and angry toward Bill. He had given her his blessing. He had believed in what she was doing. How could he
betray her and the children when he believed so strongly in her
message? She hadn't neglected him. During the times she had
seen him struggle during their marriage, she had cut back on
her speaking engagements and even canceled engagements that
had already been scheduled. She had stayed with him even
though he had been unfaithful numerous times. She had
remained loyal to him. She was committed to their marriage
and family even though he hadn't been.

Her marriage and family had meant everything to her. Her
husband and children had always been the central focus of her
life. She had been obsessed with walking with integrity. She
would have preferred to stay at home than to live a lie or to
speak a lie to people who trusted her to give them the truth.
To her, it was God who had commanded her to live a pure life,
one of truth and of principle. She was to be set apart. She was
called to live a life beyond reproach, for if anyone had found a
reason to doubt her character, her message would mean nothing. She had guarded her reputation with pride. It had been a
reputation she had worked very hard to reestablish and one that
she never wanted to relinquish. She spent much of her time
telling people to live a pure life. To do what was noble and vir-
tuous. She would never be able to speak with conviction. She
would no longer be able to tell the truth that she knew God
wanted her to speak if she were going through her own divorce.

Her own failed marriage. Her ministry was over. She knew it was, and there would be no turning back.

With that knowledge, she sought the security of her horses again. She needed the feeling of stability. When she had been a child, she had needed her horses, and as an adult, she needed everything that her horses gave her even more than when she had been a little girl riding away on her horse to forget. She didn't know how or when it would come to pass, she just had the feeling it would, and she wanted to do everything in her power to have that feeling of sitting on top of the horse, leading it. No matter what, the horse following her movements. She being one with its movements. Seeing the creation of God in the strength of its gait, the majesty of its stature. Tina drifted off to sleep as she dreamed of riding through green pastures, her hair flowing , her face brushed by the wind.

Chapter Thirty

Tina had to sit down as she put down the receiver. She was almost weak with the joy and amazement of the news she had just received. She smiled at the picture of her beautiful black stallion hanging on the wall beside her. The very expensive and powerful horse that had been a gift. A much too generous one, but a gift for which her gratitude was undying because she had received an incredible opportunity to be surrounded by her horses again. Tina remembered the moment she had first seen the horse. She had never imagined he would be hers.

The chance meeting had all begun with Tina simply thumbing through a popular horse magazine as she did from time to time. She would look through every magazine she could find, dreaming of the day when she could own a horse again. On one day in particular, Tina had come across a classified advertisement for a mare named Morning Dove. The name had caught her eye, boosting her curiosity enough to call the number listed. Tina had picked up the phone and had instantly made a connection on the other end of the line. She and the woman, Carol, who wanted to sell the mare immediately began a conversation about their faith in God, their love for horses, and the fact that Tina was anxious to buy another horse as soon as she could afford one.

When Tina had been in Duluth, Minnesota at a speaking engagement, she had looked up her new friend, Carol, had rented a car, and had driven to see her in the next town. They had spent the day talking about horses, Tina dreaming of the one she would someday own. Carol had shown her a video of a woman whom she knew named Lori Humphrey who bred Arabian horses. Tina had been awestruck. "Those are the most beautiful horses I have ever seen in my life."

"That's going to be your horse," Carol had said with a giggle.

Tina had laughed. "Yeah, right. I want a horse, but that's a twenty-five thousand dollar horse. I don't have that kind of money to spend on a horse."

Tina had not thought again of the horse until later when she received a call from Carol. Carol relayed to her that Lori had read Tina's story in *Focus on the Family* and needed to speak with her. Tina called Lori immediately. She was impatient to talk to Lori because of her extensive knowledge of horses. Lori was considered one of the best breeders in the country. Tina quickly dialed the number that Carol had given her.

"Hello?"

"Lori? This is Tina. I'm a friend of Carol."

"Hi, Tina. I read your story, and I want you come to Michigan. I want to give you a horse."

Tina had excitedly boarded the plane on the first available flight to Michigan. She remembered looking out the window of the plane. In her mind, she had gone back to the time she had ridden as a kid. The palomino stallion. She smiled remembering again. When she had been six years old, her father had sat her on top of a palomino stallion. She had ridden around the pasture as if she had spent her life on a horse. She had never been fearful of them. She felt a oneness with them, a comfort, and a peace.

She would escape the turmoil in her home by riding away on her stallion. Her whole life had changed when she lost her horses. She had found a different escape but not one quite so innocent and freeing as being on the back of a horse. She remembered when her dad had to sell her horses. How disappointed she had been. How she had felt that the most important thing in her life had been taken from her. She never imagined that she would ever own a horse again; she was being given one of the most treasured gifts that she could imagine. She felt even more restored as if God were giving her back part of the joy of her childhood, the childhood she had not been allowed. She remembered being on the plane, going to get her horse, looking into the clouds imagining that perhaps, God was pleased with her and had begun to reward her for her repentance and her duty to Him. Her heavenly Father was giving her back one of the most meaningful ways that she had worshipped Him as a child without even realizing she had. In admiring God's handiwork, she had been nurtured as a child by her Heavenly Father without even realizing who He was.

Tina remembered stepping off the plane to meet Lori. A woman who in Tina's estimation had been the holder of the dream that Tina had guarded in her heart since her teen years — since the loss of her beloved horses. Certainly she had had a strong affinity for the horses she had ridden when she was a child, but the horse that Lori wanted to give her was more symbolic than real to her. The horse symbolized a returning to the part of her youth that had brought her peace. The part that had let her escape the madness of reality. The part that when she lost it, she lost her means of finding a peace outside of herself. In all of her inner struggle, when she was atop a horse — any horse, she had power. She had the power of the horse. The muscles, the freedom, the tamed but unpredictable spirit of an animal. The spirit that she was able to tame although she had not succeeded in her youth in taming her own spirit.

Her heart was racing as she walked out to meet her benefactor, this woman whom she had never met, the woman who wanted to give her such a significant emblem of all that she had lost in her adolescence. The woman who had come to her at a time when Tina felt as if she had given all the emotional strength that she could compose to so many people who had lost as she had. The moment had been her recompense.

Tina remembered following Lori out to the barn. The only word that came to Tina was "Wow." "Wow." She said the word over and over again. Stalls and stalls full of Arabian horses. Some of the most beautiful horses she had ever seen. They were strong, sleek, beautiful horses. Bred by one of the best breeders in the world.

Lori led Tina to the stall that housed a beautiful chestnut stallion.

"He's yours."

"What? That's not possible. I can't…"

"If you'd like another one, take your pick.

Tina laughed. She had only dreamed of owning a horse as magnificent as the one she was being given. Her horse. "Wow."

When they went back inside, Lori sat down at the table and began to tell Tina the real reason why she wanted her to have one of her horses. She had read about Tina's story — the story of the woman who had tried to abort her daughter and had not succeeded. She was touched by the story of Tina's transformation. She was particularly touched by Tina's sacrifice in devoting her life to the cause of saving children, for she, herself, was unable to conceive. She and her husband had been unsuccessful in conceiving a child, and she wanted desperately to be a mother. There had been something about the story that had moved her. Something about the sense of gratitude it evoked in her for what Tina was doing. It was somehow a way of rewarding Tina for her sacrifice in trying to protect the unborn.

Lori went on to describe her own love for children and the way that she used her horses to touch children who were in need. Tina had always believed that she could see God's creation through her horses. She knew that God could speak to others, particularly children, the way He had spoken to her —

through His creation. Lori believed the concept as well and had given many horses to be used in ministries as well as to individual people whom she had felt would benefit from the strength and loyalty of a horse.

Tina was particularly moved by the idea that Lori and her husband had been unsuccessful in adopting a child. They would have been wonderful parents. They had so much to offer. Adoption. Tina never really thought about adoption in the same way after the day that she had heard Lori's story.

Tina had thought of giving Heidi up for adoption, and although she had never regretted keeping Heidi, she had never realized that there were people like Lori and her husband who were so desperate for children. Tina thought of all of the women who were terminating pregnancies when there were people like Lori and her husband who were dreaming of holding a baby in their arms. Of nurturing it. Caring for it. Loving it. All of the couples who were craving the chance to be parents, who had doors closed and opportunities denied because of abortion and because of nine months that many women refused to sacrifice.

Tina knelt beside Lori and they both prayed. They prayed to God for the chance for Lori to be a mother. They prayed and believed that God would send Lori and her husband a baby. And He answered.

Lori sounded ecstatic on the phone. She and her husband were holding their children in their arms. They received the opportunity to adopt two children from Russia. Lori and her husband were finally parents. Only months after Lori had fulfilled a dream for Tina, she had received her ultimate dream come true.

Chapter Thirty-One

Tina stood in front of a church in Michigan saying the words for the second time that morning. The pastor had asked her to speak at three different assemblies. *My daughter survived a botched abortion.* She never felt as if she were simply going through the motions. Even after everything she had been through, speaking was the hardest. Opening herself up. Being constantly reminded of her past mistakes. Having the world around her judge her actions and her heart. Her having to be honest about the kind of person she had been. She felt the pain that her testimony gave her from deep within. She had already told her story two times that morning to two different groups within the church. She was awaiting her third chance to tell her story, this time, to the entire congregation. *My daughter survived a botched abortion.* She felt as if she were forcing the words. She was pulling them out from the deepest parts of her soul and after the second time, she was bare. She couldn't pull them out the third time.

She kept telling herself she had to. There was no other way. She had a life-changing message. There could be one woman in that congregation who needed to have her life transformed. Perhaps she was contemplating abortion. Perhaps she already had the appointment. Perhaps she was like Tina, and no one had ever told her abortion was wrong. Perhaps there was a woman who had chosen abortion and was unable to live with the fact that she had terminated the life of her child. Perhaps there was a woman living in denial, being held back by stuffing into her soul the remorse and pain she felt. There could be several women in that one congregation who needed to hear the message, and Tina had to tell them. Tina had been pulled aside by women who were members of churches. Women active in churches who were living with the guilt of aborting a child. They all had the same thought that there was no way out of their pain. They had destined themselves for a lifetime of self-tormenting, self-punishing behavior. After they had heard Tina's story, the most surprising part of all to them was that Tina had been forgiven and thus had found a way of forgiving herself. Tina had been confronted by many women who believed that God could never forgive them for aborting a child so how would they ever forgive themselves? Their lives lacked peace because they continually punished themselves, never allowing God's forgiveness to fill their hearts. Tina could see the torment like a veil that they had learned to carry in an almost comfortable way as if the punishment was their only destiny. Tina had prayed and ministered to many of these women and had seen God take the veil from their faces and replace the self-torment with peace. Peace that they had felt contrition for their wrongdoing. They, like Tina, had seen that they had sinned against God and had finally asked God to heal their burden, their broken hearts, and their sin. As painful and physically demanding the task was, she had no choice. There were women, men, mothers, fathers, perhaps even grandparents who needed to find forgiveness.

She had seen men and women in church who had come to her weeping with guilt because they had supported a girlfriend, a wife, a daughter, or a friend in their decision to have an abortion. Perhaps they hadn't tried to dissuade them enough. Another may have driven their girlfriend, friend, or sister to the clinic. In whatever way, she had seen the guilt of abortion touch more than the women who had experienced the abortion first-hand. Grandparents grieved over lost grandchildren.

Fathers over their child that they had not chosen to abort. She knew that 36 million babies had been aborted since Roe vs. Wade, and the number of people who were affected by abortion multiplied exponentially when mothers, fathers, families, and friends were all taken into the toll. She could only imagine how many members of this very congregation in front of which she stood had been touched by the secret. The secret that people always kept when abortion touched them.

She knew the pain of post-abortion syndrome. She had finally gone through post-abortion counseling through Women in Ramah at the Spartanburg Crisis Pregnancy Center. Although she believed that she had received divine healing from God, she felt the post-abortion counseling completely release her from the bonds that had held her back in her life. She had been released from the subconscious memories which had kept her from having a completely victorious life. She had not enjoyed the counseling. She had pulled up all of the selfishness that had caused her to choose abortion. She was forced to come to terms with the kind of woman she had been. She had looked at how, although she had believed for much of her life that the abortions had not influenced her life, the loss of her children had affected her in a more profound way than she had ever imagined. The experience had not been a pleasant one, but it had been a powerful one — one that she believed was essential to help women not only to heal but to experience the selfishness that had caused the decision, to feel remorse for the decision, and then to find forgiveness for the choices that had brought them to the point of desperation. She knew the power of unresolved sin. She knew that it could put one's life on hold as the regret and pain festered in the deepest part of the heart and that unresolved sin could only lead to more sin and more bondage to the past. She had found a way to be truly repentant so that she could let go.

After all the years had passed and after the forgiveness she had experienced through God as well as the forgiveness she had to find for herself and her family, she had imagined that the strain of remembering all of the events and choices of her life would go away. She had felt that her maturity in her faith had been enhanced through her resolution of the abortions as well as through the strength that the pain of her divorce eventually brought her. But the pain was still there. Every time she told the story. The same words over and over. Not only did the words not become old and stale, they seemed to gain a sort of force as she repeated them. And she must repeat them again.

She gave the sacrifice she knew she had to offer and pulled the story out one final time. She never heard from any women who were touched by her message, but somehow she knew that with the intensity of what she had to say that morning, there had been at least one life touched that day, and she could go home with the resolve in her heart that she had been called. For whatever reason, she promised to continue the ministry she had chosen to leave. She had no other choice.

CHAPTER THIRTY-TWO

She couldn't discount the idea that God had blessed her. She had finally found a husband who loved her. Tina smiled as she thought of their whirlwind courtship. She realized shortly after they had started dating that Greg was the man with whom she wanted to spend her life.

Every Wednesday morning, Tina would attend a devotional at the office where she worked, and every Wednesday morning she had seen the same man who would play his guitar and sing. Tina had noticed him, thought he was attractive, but imagined that he must be married. Her sentiments changed the morning she was approached by her boss.

"Tina, I know I always tell you to be cautious about dating because of your children. But I think you should go out with Greg. I think there's something there. He's a good guy and you two have a lot in common."

Tina was surprised that her boss was even suggesting that she try out a relationship with someone. He had always been so protective of her and of her children. She trusted him deeply.

Tina's curiosity was heightened. She had begun studying Greg more carefully. She had always noticed him, but never imagining he could be single, she had seen him merely as a friend. Looking at him from another perspective gave her an interest in getting to know him better.

Greg invited Tina out to dinner. They talked for hours. They talked about their hopes for the future, what they wanted from life, and the importance of their faith. Tina knew immediately that she loved him. She had never felt so comfortable talking to a man. She had never felt so passionately for someone and had imagined that she never would. After a whirlwind courtship, one night before he left her apartment, Greg asked Tina if they could pray together.

"God, everything inside of me tells me that this is the woman with whom I want to spend the rest of my life. Please lead and guide us both in the right direction. In Your name I pray, Amen."

Tina was filled with excitement at the prospect of finding the first man with whom she felt she had truly belonged. They shared much in common, and they had an immediate bond that was unlike any she had ever experienced, but, at the same time, was completely comfortable to her.

The most telling moment of the connection that they shared happened one night soon after they had begun dating. Greg had his guitar resting on his knee and began strumming. He began singing. "It's time to make a choice, now which will it be. I can't choose for you and you can't choose for me." The song astounded Tina. It was a song about choice and choosing either life or death for one's soul. Tina sat motionless throughout the song. When he finished singing, Tina asked, "Where did that song come from?"

"I wrote it."

"When?"

"1987." Tina had known then more than ever. If she had ever had a doubt that she and Greg were supposed to be together, at the moment she heard the song, all of her doubts had dissipated.

Greg had gone to spend a weekend in Atlanta at a Promise Keepers convention to pray and fast for God's guidance in his relationship with Tina. When he returned, he asked Tina to marry him. After a short three month courtship, they were married in a ceremony that took one week to plan but to Tina was one of the most extravagant nights of her life.

Because of their short engagement, Tina and Greg spent a lot of time working through their differences. Their first year of marriage had been spent discovering each other. It was almost like they were just getting to know each other. They had to learn each other's idiosyncrasies and then had to find a way to accept each other's faults. Since they hadn't spent much time together, much of their time in the beginning of their marriage was difficult, but their commitment and love saw them through the initial demanding moments of their marriage.

Tina also found her dream of working with animals not only through rediscovering her horses, but she was also given the opportunity to work as a veterinary technician for a local animal hospital. Jacob and Stephanie were both in school, and she had found a part-time position so that she could be at home before they arrived home from school.

Through her experiences with animals, Tina was learning more and more about life. About how people viewed life. How creatures suffer. Tina knew in her heart that God wants humans to take care of animals. And if God cared so much for animals she knew how much more God cared for human beings. She realized through seeing the suffering of animals, that the suffering of people must be just as common. She needed then more than ever to refocus her energies not only on saving animals but also on helping people again. She was committed, Greg was supportive, and she began to feel once again that she had a calling.

In a way, she felt that a part of her calling was right where she was in her career at the veterinary hospital. Working with animals was the time in her life when she was learning the most about life. By watching the vet pull out the dead kittens from the mother cat's womb. By watching old animals be euthanized. By watching animals die while all she could do was stand beside them and whisper reassuring words. She knew how saddened she had become by the death of animals, by watching a cat miscarry, or by watching owners lose their devoted pets. She would cry on occasion unable to withhold her sadness for some of the situations.

One spring day, a woman came screeching into the clinic with her dog in the back of the truck. He was lying there unconscious, his feet already cold. He was already in shock. The middle-aged woman was frantic.

"We can't lose our dog. This is my husband's favorite dog. We can't lose anymore. My husband is dying of cancer. We had to file for bankruptcy, and now we're going to lose our dog."

Tina knew that if she stayed in the presence of this woman, she would not be able to guard her composure. She wouldn't necessarily be crying for the dog, although seeing an animal suffer was tragic. She would weep for this woman and her circumstances that she couldn't quite understand. She couldn't understand how one woman could be so distraught. To have lost so much. Tina asked God to put His hands on the woman to comfort her, strengthen her, and be with her. The dog passed away minutes after they brought him in.

Tina loved the idea that she was making a difference. She especially worked hard to find homes for dogs who were no longer wanted by their owners. She imagined that although the animal may have simply been a nuisance to one family, it could be a blessing to another.

Tina was also given opportunities to share the story of her life to try to help people. One morning, a seventeen-year-old intern had come into the clinic to learn about being a veterinarian. She had always wanted to become one, but wanted to shadow an actual veterinarian for a couple of days to be sure of her lifetime commitment to caring for animals.

Tina had looked at her. Seventeen. She thought back to when she was seventeen. She, too, had had aspirations of becoming a veterinarian. She had dreamed of spending her life working with animals. But she had chosen a different road. She had chosen to be sexually active at an age where girls were supposed to be finding out who they are. She had been giving her most precious gift to a guy that she hadn't even been sure she loved. And as a result of her choices, she had been forced to grow up way to soon and to give up on her dreams, her goals, and her ambitions. She had given up her social life. Her teen years had been shortened, and her life had taken a turn away from the excitement of finding a career, going to college, discovering her passions. Instead, she had spent her teen years working in a factory in order to buy diapers and pay for daycare. She never regretted being Heidi's mother. She loved her daughter and adored her grandchild, but she couldn't help but tell the young girl how much easier life was without complicating it with sex outside of marriage.

"I wish I had been more focused. Find out what you want to do and do it. Don't get distracted. Keep going. Right after you graduate from high school, go on to college, and then on to vet school. Never lose your focus."

Tina held back from telling the girl all she wanted to say—everything she had told her children. She told them daily that relationships with the opposite sex are reserved for only when they have their careers established and they know who they are. And sex was only appropriate in the context of a loving marriage. Sex any other time would only bring distractions, pain, or even an aborted child. She had realized the ramifications of a life with no guidance, no discipline, and no passion. She saw the results of her promiscuity in her later relationships. She had regretted deeply not saving her virginity for marriage. It was as if she had given a piece of her heart to someone she had barely known and she had created a child with someone with whom she had no lasting relationship — a man who would abandon his own daughter. She had seen the results of a young woman's life who had spent carefree days running from responsibility to the point that she was forced into a responsibility much more taxing than any duties from which she had been running. And she knew more than anyone how mistakes could be seared into a memory for a lifetime, and forgiveness could bring relief but could never change the ramifications of bad decisions.

She knew of regret. Regret over an abortion that could have resulted in stripping her of a beautiful, caring, compassionate daughter as well as a glorious granddaughter. Regret over two other abortions. Regret over a lost marriage. And although she had found a way to forgive herself, she had come to take responsibility for all that had happened in her life for the choices she had made. She had found a way to be freed from the haunting of her past, but she hadn't found a way of going back to change her decisions. What she had done was done, and she had learned to make the best of the life that she had fought against odds to build.

She knew that she was forgiven by God. She had forgiven herself, but the act of aborting a child had affected her in many ways she scarcely understood. Particularly dealing with an abortion, although unsuccessful, at such a tender age, had molded and shaped her in ways she couldn't imagine. The decisions that she had made in her youth had made her into an adult and although she could forgive herself, her soul would forever be changed and marked by the idea that she had not always lived a pure life.

She was certain that she was the recipient of many blessings. She had three beautiful children, a beautiful granddaughter and another grandchild to be born at any moment, and a husband who loved her. Her treasured horses had come back into her life once again. She knew that God was blessing her, for all of the desires of her heart were coming to her one by one. She hadn't had all of her children under the most ideal circumstances, but at the same time, they were her ultimate blessing. She had a marriage that ended in divorce but in the midst of their troubled relationship, two beautiful children had come into her life. And even through the pain of divorce, she had seen herself become stronger, more confident, and assured in her faith. She had changed from a woman who had three abortions to a woman who fought and struggled to stop other women from falling into the same trap. She had realized her dream of working to help save animals, the dream of her youth that she imagined would never be realized. But most of all, amidst all of the turmoil, the bad decisions, and the pain that resulted from her choices, she had been given peace. God had restored her heart. He had made a way for her to experience the peace that she never believed she would find, and as she looked out across the pasture at the beauty of the land, her horses grazing in the pasture, and the sun slowly rising over the mountains, she thought of how her life had evolved. The story of a life that had begun more than a little off track had become a soul that was at peace. At peace with her past and hopeful for the future.

CHAPTER THIRTY-THREE

Unlike most mothers, Tina was consciously aware of two moments that had signaled the birth of her firstborn child. The first was April of 1978, the day she had left the clinic thinking she had terminated an unwanted pregnancy. The second was the day she had actually given birth, a cool fall November day. A day she had recalled just as lucidly. The outcome of the two days were equally significant. But on this day, in particular, her focus was more on the former. Perhaps it was the weather. Perhaps it was the thought of her new grandchild. The reminder of youth and the youthfulness she had experienced before that moment on April 4, 1978, the same youth that had disappeared from her that very day not long after she had stepped from her car — perhaps by coercion, perhaps by her own will — she still wasn't completely sure. But as she sped along Highway 123 toward Greenville, the initial force seemed less important than the outcome. The glorious outcome who lay in his crib waiting to be held by his grandmother, to be spoiled in a way that only grandmothers can. To be loved the way only children can be loved. Her thoughts were consumed with babyhood and motherhood and what actually constituted the two. And had April 4, 1978 been varied by even a millisecond, she would have never been given the title that she cherished most, and she would have never been driving to her daughter's apartment at that very moment filled with the anxious anticipation that only grandparents can know.

But she couldn't think of the birth of her grandchild without thinking of the days of her daughter's births. The first being a rebirth of sorts. Certainly a rebirth for Tina. A chance to right a wrong. Truly symbolic of second chances even if it had taken her several more chances to take that second chance. The second birth being nothing short of a miracle.

How funny, she thought. Funny in the ironic sense, not at all in the comedic one. How funny to be driving down the street on a spring day. How odd and completely different the feeling of a woman in her forties. A woman who had seen much more than a girl who was seventeen. It had been a day like the one she was experiencing. The sort of spring day that was made strangely hot by the fiery rays of the sun coming so quickly after the coolness of the winter. The rays made their way in a sort of shocking way through the cold to penetrate the chill of spring.

That day in April. As much as she tried to remove the memory from the deepest crevices of her recollection, the smell in the air, the glare of the sun, the black of the pavement, all of her senses brought her back to that day. The day that could never be replaced by the birth. No. They were one in the same, inseparable; for the day of the birth of her daughter could have never existed had the miracle not changed the course of her own little destiny. A tiny little baby had had her life decided in the miracle of one moment — the memory of which Tina had learned to recall and repress at will, the way some people who experience traumatic events seem to learn to live with the circumstances that follow those events.

The irony was mostly the weather. For that day, the day that she was recalling into her memory, the spring day that signaled renewing had seemed more to her like the last day of autumn, the beginning of a cold, dark winter. The same way the leaves would fall from the trees and the branches would take on a look of death. That day, April 4, 1978 had seemed, on that day anyway, to symbolize death. But she would learn that that day had symbolized more about life than any other day except for perhaps the birth of her children. The very day that had seemed so lifeless would be the day that would end up being the most life-giving. The most transforming. The most miraculous. And on a day like today, she had lived the seemingly tortuous moment that had ended in her driving on this very road that very day with the same promise of spring. The reassured promise of life it had taken her half a lifetime to find.

Tina sighed and allowed her mind to go back to that day. Perhaps the pain was too great or maybe the emotions of that day too raw to revive. She rarely allowed herself to venture back to that day. But on the day that she was celebrating the birth of her grandchild, she couldn't keep herself from transforming her mind from a woman to the girl that with one less miracle would have never evolved to the woman she was at that very moment. Tina felt the tears as they fell. It was as if, in her memory, she was watching a girl that she barely knew and at the same time it was a girl that she knew very well. She cried for that girl.

Tina continued her drive. She hadn't known exactly what to wear that morning. She only knew that she would be working. Heidi needed her help. She smiled when she imagined what an independent woman Heidi had become compared to the child Tina herself had been as she groped with Heidi's diapers and fumbled with her bottles desperately needing her own mother's guidance just to care for her.

Her final destination reassumed her thoughts, her happy ones, as she continued down 123 into downtown Greenville. The downtown that had been revived to attract families. To attract new business. How downtown Greenville had changed from when she had been a teenager. She passed Main Street. The center of town was bustling with the emergence of new banks, businesses, restaurants, coffeehouses. She saw businessmen in their suits, construction workers changing the facade of buildings to allow for new commerce. She saw children licking ice cream cones. Centuries away from the times she had cruised downtown, her car packed full of friends. Drugs, alcohol, rock music. *The days of the foolish,* she thought. She had known so little for someone who was forced into deciding so much.

It usually happened that immediately as she thought of her youth, she would automatically go back to her childhood. Her youth had been so haphazard. So unkempt as sorts and she always tried to go back to find reasons, justifications. What ifs. What if her parents hadn't divorced? What if she had not been stripped of her passion for horses? What if. What if. What if. She would temper her what-ifs always with, *But look at Heidi, Stephanie, Jacob. And Greg.* What ifs would erase them and so she would decide to stop the what ifs because she couldn't have changed many parts of her life for fear that she would have missed out on one of her children or her husband. But her curiosity continued to grab her as she searched, as most people do, for reasons why. Reasons why her life and her actions had taken such erratic sharp turns rather than a straight, easy path. She searched until she came to the beginning. The beginning of her life. Like a maze she imagined her life and her paths and dead-ends where she had had to find the right path again and why? Why had she taken so many bad turns? Where did her undoing begin? But as her car crept to the entrance of Heidi's residence, the why seemed much less important.

Tina signaled and pulled into the parking lot of Heidi's apartment complex. She stepped out of the car and walked into the apartment.

Tina took Dylan in her arms. He was beautiful. His skin was perfectly polished. Unscathed by the elements. No blemishes. No lines. No wrinkles. Completely new. He represented everything that was innocent and hopeful. He had no iniquitous thoughts. He was absent of any memories that would haunt him. He was born without any notions of ill will, regret, or broken promises. He was void of the knowledge of all things evil. Full of the tender innocence that only newborns possess.

She was mesmerized by his little miniature hands. His feet. His toes. The smell of baby. The sweet, sleepy smell of a baby.

Tina began to cry. Cry as she always cried when she held a baby. Baby Jacob. Not her Jacob. Thinking of her own baby Jacob would bring tears of joy. Tears of nostalgia for the child she had carried, raised, and nurtured. These tears were tears of complete mourning. She was mourning the Baby Jacob because he was a soul. She was thinking of Baby Jacob as a symbol. Rather than being clean, powdered in baby powder, and being carefully swaddled in a blanket by his mother, Baby Jacob had died. He had died a painful death in the womb of his mother, left in the trash to be buried by strangers. Baby Jacob was more than Baby Jacob. He was a symbol. A symbol of a society that had seemingly gone mad. Allowing the lives of babies like the precious angelic gift from God that she held in her hands to be terminated at will. A society that condoned and supported the abortions of babies like the one that she was cuddling in her arms.

Don't all babies deserve what Dylan has? A mother who cares for him? A father who provides for him? A grandmother who finds his very existence an absolute miracle?

They do deserve the same. All of the babies. Only many of them get the worst. Before they are even allowed to get a glimpse of the face of the woman in whose womb they grew. Before they are ever allowed to swing in the park or take their first plunge into a pool. They never get the chance to be rocked to sleep as sweet lullabies soothe their cries. They will never hear the heartbeats of their fathers as they pat their babies backs and walk around the house whispering "Shhh. Don't cry. Daddy's here." They will never hear the crash of the ocean waves or see the sunset behind the mountains. The kind of sunset where a child says "Mommy, where does the sun go?" They are never given the chance to take their first breath. Their first painful breath signaling their entrance into the world with all the promise and hope of the future. Those babies are never awarded their birthright for their birth is taken from them. Taken from them by the ones who had chosen to perform the act of making their existence possible.

She was burdened by the funeral honoring Baby Jacob. She thought of him every time she held a baby in her arms. She thought of his little fingers and toes, his soft skin with little burn marks, his little nose. She held him everyday in her heart. She thought of him everyday, wept at least one tear for him everyday. But she needed to be broken. She needed to keep a humble spirit in remembering her own decisions about abortion. She also needed to remember the cause for which she was fighting. She needed a reason to face the humiliation and the stress of admitting her secrets to the world. God wanted her to be broken over the babies who had died. She needed to see that abortion was not a political issue or a women's rights issue. It was an issue about the life of babies. Real babies. Babies like little Dylan who was gently squirming as if trying to snuggle against her chest.

Suddenly her grandchild became heavy. Heavy in a spiritual sense as if she were holding in her arms all of those babies. Those babies who were never given a chance to breathe, to feel love, to feel safe. All of them. And at that moment, her burden was once again renewed just as it had been when she saw the sweet innocence of Baby Jacob. Just as it was when she buried the baby in Alabama. Only the baby that she held in her arms was a symbol of life. Life that she wanted to help save, just as God had saved Heidi's life.

Her gratitude was undying. Undying in the sense that she had a connection to God, a daily reminder of the miracle that God had performed in her life. She had had other plans for Heidi. But God stepped in and held His hand between her baby and what she had wanted done. He had saved her baby from her own mother. He had kept the suction machine from touching her. Her Heidi. The Heidi that had given up her childhood and teenage years to help save other children. The Heidi who had spoken out and said, "I'm living proof that those babies are real." She gave up much, suffered much, and sacrificed even in the face of knowing that her mother had tried to abort her. She was the hero in the story. The baby that had used God's strength to be born in the most impossible of situations and then stepped up as a child speaking with wisdom and courage in the face of hate to be the spokesperson for the unborn. Without Heidi many more babies would have been aborted. Because of Heidi, many lives were saved. Many mothers were saved the torture of knowing that they had aborted their own children. And all of these small miracles happened because of the one miracle of Heidi.

Heidi had brought life to Tina as well. Tina knew that Heidi had been the reason for the change in her own life. Without Heidi, Tina would have never experienced her own miracle. The miracle of faith. The transformation that could have come only in knowing God. Heidi had brought life and joy to Tina and to a world — to everyone who had ever heard the story of the miracle of her birth.

If Heidi had not been protected, had not been given the strength to fight and win, there would have been no Mychaela and no Dylan. Tina, her family, and the world would have been less rich without the curiosity and wonder in the eyes of little Mychaela. The world would have seen less tender innocence without the little soul of Dylan having been born.

She wondered what they would accomplish. How many lives would they touch throughout their lifetimes? And their children, grandchildren, an entire lineage scarcely to be in existence had it not been for the miracle? Tina wondered what all of the aborted babies who had died had been destined to do. Would there have been a President, a great evangelist, a wonderful mother, a schoolteacher, a farmer, a great leader, or a great father? Who knew what the world had missed without these children? Tina knew for she had three reminders that she saw everyday. She knew what she would have missed had the abortion been successful. Heidi, Mychaela, and Dylan. She knew that she would have never been the same without their warm hearts filling her own with love. Love that, short of a miracle, she would have missed.